BAPTISM OF DESIRE or BLOOD
(A Defense in Brief
Ad Majorem Dei Gloriam)
Revised and Expanded

By Steven Speray

VERITAS

DEFENDING THE CATHOLIC FAITH
2009

Baptism of Desire or Blood
(A Defense in Brief
Ad Majorem Dei Gloriam)

Copyright 2009 by Steven Speray

ISBN: 978-0-578-03408-9

Published by Confiteor
P.O. Box 83
Versailles, KY 40383
www.catholictopgun.com

OUR LADY OF THE ROSARY CHAPEL
Bishop Robert F. McKenna, O.P.
15 Pepper St.
Monroe, Connecticut
Tel. (203) 261-8290

January 8, 2009

Dear Steven,

I'm sorry I haven't been able to write sooner after reading your book on Baptism of Desire. I'm ever inundated with work – doubly so at Christmas – that prevents me the luxury of reading and studying, for which I have to steal time!

Your work is a fine job of both research and presentation, covering all aspects of the question. The supplementary material is very good and interesting too. But while so well defending Baptism of Desire, you seem almost to apologize in a way for it in calling it a miracle and seemingly emphasizing its rarity. Like the sacrament itself, it is indeed something supernatural and to that extent a miracle of grace, but the Lord alone knows how many souls are actually saved by Baptism of Desire, being inculpably ignorant of the need for the sacrament. More perhaps than we may think.

Anyway, you have thoroughly demonstrated the authorities for its pertaining to the Ordinary Magisterium of the Church and therefore infallible Catholic doctrine. I hope you will find a publisher for the book. God reward you in any case!

In Christ,

Bishop McKenna

Table of Contents

The Principle Understanding of the Doctrine of Baptism of Desire and Blood
    - What Baptism of Desire and Blood is and isn't........... 11

The Different Positions of Objections to the doctrine of BOD and BOB

    - 4 major positions of objections.............................. 17

The Official Teaching of the Church -
    The Council of Trent, The Council of Florence and the Catechisms of Trent, Pope St. Pius X, and the Plenary Council of Baltimore... 19

The Law of the Church - 1917 Code of Canon Law.............. 25

The Practice of the Church – The Breviary........................ 29

The Teaching of Popes – Direct and Indirect Teachings....... 31

The unofficial 1949 Letter.. 37

IN SUMMARY.. 39

The 33 Objections to Baptism of Desire and/or Blood:

    1. John 3:5 should be understood "as it is written"....... 41
    2. God doesn't command impossibilities..................... 41
    3. Miracles prove absolute necessity of Baptism.......... 44
    4. St. Alphonsus Liquori's error................................. 47
    5. Pope St. Siricius and his Letter to Himerius............ 48
    6. Trent's Canons 2, 4, and 5.................................... 49
    7. Trent's Canon 4 specifically................................... 51
    8. One Baptism not Three.. 52
    9. 1917 Canon Law is not infallible and in error........... 52
    10.   Athanasian Creed.. 53
    11.   Pope St. Leo the Great, dogmatic letter to Flavian, Council of Chalcedon... 54
    12.   Noah's ark had no exceptions........................... 55

13. The doctrine is not defined, therefore, we are free to disagree............ 55
14. Implicit desire would imply that Protestants, Muslims, Jews, pagans, etc could be saved in their religion.....57
15. Baptism of Desire is an evolution rather than the development of a doctrine................................. .59
16. It is theological opinion at best, so it need not be believed...................................60
17. The example of Sodom and Gomorrah argues against it..............61
18. Baptism of Blood was condemned by Popes Pelagius and Eugene IV..62
19. Pope Clement XI, in his statement to missionaries, implied that it was not possible............................ 63
20. The Gospel is not necessary if Baptism of Desire is true...................................64
21. It would be harder for Catholics to be saved........65
22. *Apostolicam Sedem*, attributed to Pope Innocent II, is probably a forgery. It has no real authority since we can't be sure who actually wrote it......................................66
23. Pope Innocent III's letter to a Bishop Berthold of Metz on August 28, 1206, is not binding.............................67
24. *Singulari Quidem* of Pope Pius IX was writing about hope not salvation itself..67
25. Pope Pius IX, in *Quanto Conficiamur Moerore*, was not teaching Baptism of Desire.................................68
26. Catechism of St. Pius X is clearly in error and should be rejected.. 70
27. Pope Leo XIII in *Satis Cognitum* condemned the idea that one can be in the soul and not body of the Church.................................. .71
28. An incorrect conclusion is drawn from the story about St. Alban and his guard...72
29. To say un-Baptized infants can be saved by Baptism of Blood goes directly against the teaching of Pope Eugene IV and the Council of Florence................................. 73
30. God allowed the war to stop short of Vatican I to keep it from falling into error by defining Baptism of Desire and Blood... .73

31. The Church may have not condemned those false teachings from the catechisms and the saints, but that doesn't mean the doctrine is true............................ 75
32. A person may obtain Justification but cannot attain Salvation unless he receives the Sacraments............ 77
33. Salvation can come only through the Sacrament of Baptism is a very hard saying,
and it requires greater faith.................................... 77

APPENDIX 1 - OUTSIDE THE CHURCH THERE IS NO SALVATION.
From the Popes.. 79

APPENDIX 2 - NECESSITY OF BAPTISM AND/OR FAITH
From the Popes.. 85

APPENDIX 3 - ONE BAPTISM NOT THREE
From the Popes.. 89

APPENDIX 4 - ON LAWS AND DISCIPLINES OF THE CHURCH
Popes teach laws and disciplines of the Church are without error...91

APPENDIX 5 - BAPTISM OF DESIRE AND BLOOD
BY THE SAINTS AND DOCTORS OF THE CHURCH
Includes: a. A Private Revelation of the Great Saint Catherine of Sienna
  b. Historical examples......................... 97

APPENDIX 6 - THE FEWNESS OF THE SAVED
From Holy Writ, Popes,
Doctors of the Church and Saints..................... 113

APPENDIX 7 - STORIES OF MIRACLES
Two stories of great missionaries...................... 125

APPENDIX 8 - THE CASES THAT INVOLVE UN-BAPTIZED INFANTS
Explains what happens to them in all cases........ 131

APPENDIX 9 - THE HOLY SCRIPTURES ON THE CATHOLIC CHURCH..137

All Scripture quotes come from one of the following sources:
    Douay-Rheims,
    Confraternity (Challoner Rheims),
    Revised Standard Version Catholic Edition

All papal or saint quotes come from one of the following sources unless otherwise noted:

    The Papal Encyclicals, Claudia Carlen, Raleigh: The Peirian Press, Vol. 1 (1740-1878), Vol. 2 (1878-1903), Vol. 3 (1903-1939), Vol. 4 (1939-1958)

    The Sources of Catholic Dogma, Denzinger "Enchiridion Symbolorum", Roy J. Deferrari, 13th Edition, Loreto Publications

    Decrees of the Ecumenical Councils, Norman P. Tanner SJ, Sheed & Ward and Georgetown University Press, 1990, Vol. 1 and 2, Tanner

    The Faith of the Early Fathers, William A. Jurgens, Collegeville, MN, The Liturgical Press, 1970, Vol. 1, 2, and 3

BAPTISM OF DESIRE or BLOOD
A Defense in Brief
Ad Majorem Dei Gloriam
By Steven Speray

And they were exceedingly astonished, and said to him, "Then who can be saved?" Jesus looked at them and said, "With men it is impossible, but not with God; for all things are possible with God." Mark 10:26-27

The oft-defined dogma *Extra Ecclesiam Nulla Salus* (EENS) or outside the Church there is no salvation is a dogma that is severely misunderstood, misrepresented, and attacked.

This writing will explain and defend how EENS applies in extraordinary cases and conditions.

The Catholic Church, through Scripture and Tradition, infallibly teach that the Catholic Faith plus the Sacrament of Baptism are the means by which man enters the Church apart from no one can be saved. SEE APPENDIX 1 and APPENDIX 9

From this dogma, several questions arise. If for some reason Baptism were made impossible or faith was unknown by circumstances beyond one's control, is salvation possible? Are there any exceptions to the dogma where salvation is possible outside the Church? If it is possible for one to be saved apart from Baptism or explicit Catholic Faith, would it be contrary to the dogma EENS?

This is the subject of extraordinary cases. They can be broken down into two categories:

1. The case where one has explicit Catholic Faith or Desire where Baptism is not possible.
2. The case where one has implicit Faith or Desire where explicit faith is not possible.

The Catholic Church teaches that all men must absolutely be inside the Church to be saved, no exceptions whatsoever.

In extraordinary cases just mentioned, the doctrine of Baptism of Desire 'BOD' and/or Blood 'BOB', explains how it is possible to enter the Church without the actual Sacrament of Baptism.

The Principle Understanding of the Doctrine of Baptism of Desire and Blood

The doctrine of Baptism of Desire says that at death, provided there is faith, desire (implicit or explicit) to be baptized, and perfect contrition for all sins, one will be brought into the Church without the actual Sacrament of Water Baptism. Baptism of Blood is the doctrine that refers to those who couldn't receive the Sacrament but shed their blood for Christ.

Some BOD/BOB defenders might say that objectively one can be outside the Church but subjectively inside the Church. They mean that in the external forum, there are those who appear to be outside the Church, but aren't really. Catholics can find themselves through ignorance practicing a Protestant religion. This is true, but some mean that subjectively a Protestant is really a Catholic because of a false understanding of what the Church is, or that a non-baptized person can be inside the Church subjectively. This approach runs contrary to the Dogma of EENS and there would be no need of the doctrine of Baptism of Desire or Blood. BOD/BOB doesn't really apply to the baptized anyway, since the Sacrament of Baptism has already been administered to such persons.

Therefore, rather than running contrary to the Dogma *"Extra Ecclesiam Nulla Salus,"* the doctrine of BOD/BOB, when understood correctly, explains how the dogma applies in extraordinary cases and conditions. Thus from the above statements comes the very first objection against the doctrine of BOD/BOB. SEE ALSO OBJECTION 1

We see Christ saying to Nicodemus, *"Unless a man be born of water and Holy Spirit, he cannot enter into the Kingdom of Heaven."* (John 3:5) Later, we read in Ephesians 4 that there is, *"one Lord, one faith, one baptism."* Also, we have the teaching of the popes, councils, and saints that speak of the absolute necessity of Water Baptism to enter the Church. SEE APPENDIX 2.

Based on these teachings, the first objection says Our Lord's words are meant to apply absolutely in every case since Scripture (confirmed by popes) says there is one baptism not three. SEE APPENDIX 3 and OBJECTION 8

This objection to the doctrine of BOD/BOB is a straw-man argument because it fails to distinguish between those ordinary cases from extraordinary cases.

Water Baptism is absolutely necessary and it is the necessity of means...under ordinary conditions, which is understood as *"necessity of precept."* The Church makes proper distinctions between *"necessity of means"* and *"necessity of precept"* and between ordinary circumstances and extraordinary circumstances. Technically speaking, the phrase *"necessity of means"* is used for all circumstances.

This means all those statements from Scriptures, popes and saints fall under the rubric *"necessity of precept,"* and were meant under ordinary conditions.

Baptisms of Desire and Blood refer only to extraordinary cases and conditions.

Those who argue that this is creating a false dichotomy are failing to reconcile all of the teachings of the Church. They are isolating one side while condemning the other. This is illogical.

The proof is in the sources themselves. Several of the popes, saints, and catechisms, and even Scripture also refer to the absolute necessity of Baptism by water and yet these very same sources include exceptions in extraordinary cases. Thus, necessity of precept vs necessity of means must be distinguished.

Those who are bent on objecting to the doctrine say these sources are contradicting themselves. This is silly nonsense, because the sources are explaining the difference between the ordinary and extraordinary.

Therefore, it is false to say that outside the Church there is salvation in extraordinary conditions. This explanation goes against the dogma EENS. If someone asks, can a Jew, Muslim, or Protestant be saved? The answer is simply no, not as a Jew, Muslim, or Protestant, but they can be saved as Catholics.

It would be incorrect to say that they were saved in their religion or by their religion, for it is neither. SEE OBJECTION 14

Again, it is not how salvation might be attained outside the Church because there is no salvation outside the Church. Baptism of Desire/Blood is the explanation how those outside the Church get inside the Church immediately before or at death.

Baptism of Desire and Blood is not a defined dogma. The First Vatican Council intended to define it but was cut short because of the Franco-Prussian war. SEE OBJECTION 30 It is rather a doctrine given the name of Baptism of Desire/Blood to explain the application of the dogma EENS under extraordinary conditions.

Baptism of Desire means that it is only a possibility that one outside the Church can get inside, not that it has ever happened since we haven't a saint from Baptism of Desire. It's highly unlikely for it would appear to be a very rare event. SEE APPENDIX 6

However, there are recognized saints from Baptism of Blood. SEE PRACTICE OF THE CHURCH

This not only proves that it is possible to be saved without the Sacrament, but you must believe it since the Church is infallible in recognizing saints. SEE OBJECTION 31 and PRACTICE OF THE CHURCH.

The case of implicit desire means one who is invincibly ignorant is not saved by his invincible ignorance. Take careful note of this. Invincible ignorance does not save. It is the worst kind of handicap.

Baptism of Desire means God infuses the Catholic Faith immediately before or at death, wherefore one is no longer ignorant.

This invincible ignorance must be about the Catholic Faith for those who are not ill-willed for as St. Paul says in II Corinthians 4:3: "And if our gospel be hid, it is hid to them that are lost, In whom the god of this world (Satan) hath blinded the minds of unbelievers, that the light of the gospel of the glory of Christ, who is the image of God, should not shine unto them."

There is no such thing as an invincibly ignorant atheist as St. Paul says in Romans 1:18-20: *"For the wrath of God is revealed from Heaven against all ungodliness and injustice of those men that detain the truth of God in injustice: Because that which is known of God is manifest in them. For God hath manifested it to them. For the invisible things of him, from the creation of the world, are clearly seen, being understood by the things that are made; his external power also, and divinity: so that they are inexcusable."*

God can save anyone that pleases Him (only He knows). It is possible. See Mark 10:26-27, Luke 18:27

Since perfect contrition is required for those who can't receive Confessional absolution, then by logical extension, it would be required for Baptism of Desire if you can't receive Water Baptism.

Even perfect contrition must come from a response to God's grace. God is always working to save men provided that they are open to His grace since He desires all men to be saved. SEE OBJECTION 20

Would anyone argue that God does not give the grace for one to have perfect contrition for his sins? And since He gives it, one must be able to respond to it or why should He give it at all? SEE OBJECTION 2

Since one can respond to it by having perfect sorrow, how can God send him to hell with it? If such a one were sent to hell, what would this say about God's mercy and forgiveness?

Baptism of Desire cannot apply to one who has imperfect contrition. In other words, if a man believes all the truths of the Catholic Faith, desires the necessary Sacrament of Baptism, and is truly sorry for all his sins, not because of the primary love for God as in perfect contrition, but fears the punishment of hell due to his sins, he cannot and will not be saved by Baptism of Desire.

Baptism of Blood may not require perfect contrition.

BOD and BOB are not sacraments. The Mark of Baptism comes with the Sacrament. The Church hasn't said if those who die by BOD/BOB receive any mark. The Old Testaments Saints also do not have the Mark of Baptism. Surely, Abel, Enoch, Abraham, Isaac, Jacob, Moses, Elias, Joseph, and John the Baptist have some of the highest places in Heaven without the Mark of Baptism.

The designated terms (Baptism of Desire/Blood) are about what constitutes the possible exceptions to the Sacrament. It must necessarily fall under at the very least the universal and ordinary teaching of the Church, as it is referenced at the Council of Trent. SEE OBJECTIONS 13 and 16

Baptism of Desire, without a doubt, would take a miracle. SEE APPENDIX 6

The Different Positions of Objections to the doctrine of BOD and BOB.

1. The position that is against Baptism of Implicit Desire but not Explicit Desire and of Blood.

The problem with this position is that it already admits the possibility to be saved without the Sacrament and would have to deal with the teaching of Pope Pius IX. SEE OBJECTION 25

2. The position that is against Implicit and Explicit Desire but not of Blood.

Again, the problem admits the possibility to be saved without the Sacrament and would have to deal with the whole argument that involves statements from several popes, catechisms, and saints.

3. The position that is against Implicit and Explicit Desire and of Blood but believes it is permissible to hold or reject.

This objection will have to deal with the authority of the Church.

4. The position that is totally against BOD/BOB and believes it is heretical and not permissible to hold as a Catholic.

This objection says all those Saints and Doctors of the Church that did believe it are either material or formal heretics. It implies the Church has failed in preventing the heretical teachings to be spread through official catechisms and even in the laws of the Church. It also implies that the Church has issued harmful laws and practices.

The Official Teaching of the Church

The Council of Trent

Canons on the Sacraments in General: - (Canon 4):

*"If anyone shall say that the sacraments of the New Law are not necessary for salvation, but are superfluous, and **that although all are not necessary for every individual, without them or without the desire of them** (sine eis out eorum voto), through faith alone men obtain from God the grace of justification; let him be anathema."*
SEE OBJECTION 7

Decree on Justification - (Session 6, Chapter 4):

*"In these words a description of the justification of a sinner is given as being a translation from that state in which man is born a child of the first Adam to the state of grace and of the 'adoption of the sons' (Rom. 8:15) of God through the second Adam, Jesus Christ, our Savior and this translation after the promulgation of the Gospel cannot be effected **except through [or without] the laver of regeneration or a desire for it,** (sine lavacro regenerationis out eius voto) as it is written: "Unless a man be born again of water and the Holy Spirit, he cannot enter in the kingdom of God (John 3:5)."*
OBJECTION 32

Take notice that Trent quoted John 3:5 after speaking about a desire for baptism. SEE OBJECTION 6

Four times, The Catechism of Trent or Roman Catechism quotes Christ, *"Unless a man be born of water and Holy Spirit, he cannot enter into the Kingdom of Heaven (John 3:5)."* (pp 163, 164, 171, and 177)

The Roman Catechism was ordered by the Council of Trent to explain the Council's teachings, and was edited by St. Charles Borromeo and promulgated by Pope St. Pius V. In other words, this

Catechism is the official interpretation of the Canons of Trent along with other articles of Faith.

The official Catechism cannot teach a heresy. If it could then the Church could promulgate a lie, which is impossible. Also, if one rejects the Catechism on one point, he could never justify the use of it to prove another.

All the church fathers know the John 3:5 quote and yet nearly all, who had anything to say on the subject, teach a Baptism of Desire or of Blood. SEE APPENDIX 5

How can this be? Do they all reject Christ's teaching since it has been repeated to mean, *"As it is written"?* SEE OBJECTION 1

Are not Christ's words true?

Well, take this example: Christ says, *"unless you eat the flesh of the Son of man and drink his blood, you have no life in you."* (John 6:53 in RSV, 6:54 in CRV)

If one were to take this in the absolute literal sense, Christ would be saying that anybody who has never received Communion could not enter Heaven since there would be no life in him. This is not what Christ meant and we understand that. Yet, John 3:5 uses the same terminology. Some try to refute this by saying the word *"unless"* in John 6 is not correct. They argue that *"except"* is the better translation, which gives us a different terminology. The problem with this refutation is *"unless you" and "except ye"* ultimately mean the same thing.

Take another example: Christ says, *"judge not, and you will not be judged."* (Matt 7:1)

If one were to take this out of context and make it literally an absolute statement, then we would not have to love, or be baptized as long as we don't judge anyone, and God will not judge us to damnation. Of course this would be a silly interpretation.

Christ is using hyperbole and He employs this method several times. He is stressing the importance of our actions. As with His statement with Baptism, *"Unless a man be born of water..."* is not to be understood in every single case, according to the Church and the Fathers.

We must absolutely be baptized if Baptism is possible. It is not optional as Trent states. SEE OBJECTION 6

If you say that BOD or BOB goes against the plain teaching of Christ in John 3:5, then you must say that all those saints that also happen to be great Doctors of the Church, such as St. Augustine, St. John Chrysostom, St. Bonaventure, St. Alphonsus Liquori, St. Robert Bellarmine, St. Gregory Nanianzus, St. Bernard, St. Thomas Aquinas, St. John Damascene, St. Cyril of Jerusalem, and Venerable Bede, are all going against Our Lord's words and therefore against Christ, making them all heretics and antichrists teaching a gospel contrary to Our Lord.

The Council of Florence and the Catechisms of Trent, Pope St. Pius X, and the Plenary Council of Baltimore.

Pope Eugene IV, Council of Florence, Session 11, Feb. 4, 1442:

"Regarding children, indeed, because of danger of death, which can often take place, when no help can be brought to them by another remedy than through the sacrament of baptism, through which they are snatched from the domination of the Devil [original sin] and adopted among the sons of God, it advises that holy baptism ought not be deferred for forty or eighty days, or any time according to the observance of certain people..."

The Roman Catechism says baptism for infants should not be delayed *"Since infant children have **no other means** of **salvation** except Baptism..."* (P. 178)

Question: Why do we have these statements if there is no other remedy or means except baptism anyway? Why does it say this for infants only? SEE APPENDIX 8

The following is the answer from the Church:

The same Roman Catechism quotes four times John 3:5.

The Roman Catechism also says adults *"are not baptized at once...The delay is not attended the same danger as in the case of infants, which we have already mentioned; should any foreseen accident make it impossible for adults to be washed in the salutary waters, their intention and determination to receive Baptism and their repentance for past sins, will avail them to grace and righteousness."* (p 179)

These two statements clearly teach that, un-baptized infants cannot have SALVATION, but un-baptized Catechumens who by intention and determination could not get the Water Baptism because of some unforeseen accident can have salvation. This is clearly the reading of text as even expounded by the Church fathers.

One might say that grace and righteousness is not Heaven. If so, what does it mean? If you don't know, then the very Catechism of Trent that is used to instruct the Faithful is failing to do just that. However, we know what the Catechism means unless one is bent on rejecting the doctrine.

The Council of Florence is infallible and Trent's Catechism flows from Florence on this point.

We have *"The New St. Joseph Baltimore Catechism"*, which states:

No. 2, Q. 321 - *"How can those be saved who through no fault of their own have not received the Sacrament of Baptism.*

A. Those who through no fault of their own have not received the sacrament of Baptism can be saved through what is called baptism of blood or baptism of desire."

We also have the *"Catechism of St. Pius X"* written by Pope St. Pius X:

29 Q: But if a man through no fault of his own is outside the Church, can he be saved?

A: If he is outside the Church through no fault of his, that is, if he is in good faith, and if he has received Baptism, or at least has the implicit desire of Baptism; and if, moreover, he sincerely seeks the truth and does God's will as best he can such a man is indeed separated from the body of the Church, but is united to the soul of the Church and consequently is on the way of salvation. SEE OBJECTION 25

Does man absolutely under all circumstances have to receive water baptism to be saved?

According to the Catholic Church's official interpretation (Roman Catechism) of Christ's words, *"Unless a man be born of water..." the* answer is a resounding NO!

Lastly, great popes such a Pope St. Pius X never condemned these Catechisms. If they were teaching heresy or contrary to the faith, this pope would have done so. However, he also believed it as he clearly writes in his own catechism. SEE OBJECTION 31

The Law of the Church

Canon 1239.2 of the 1917 Code of Canon Law declares, *"catechumens who through no fault of their own, die without Baptism, are to be treated as Baptized."*

The Sacred Cannons by Rev. John A. Abbo, S.T.L., J.C.D. and Rev. Jerome D. Hannan, A.M., LL.B., S.T.D., J.C.D.

Commentary on the Code: *"The reason for this rule is that they are justly supposed to have met death united to Christ through Baptism of Desire."* SEE OJECTION 9

Why would the Church, in her own official law, say this if Baptism of Desire were not a teaching of the Church?

Also, notice that to be treated as baptized without actually being baptized means that the Church in her universal law teaches the doctrine of Baptism of Desire. If it were an error to hold to this teaching, then the Church did what it dogmatically stated that it could not do...teach a harmful error by law. SEE APPENDIX 4. The Church cannot scandalize or lead Her members into heresy and error through Her laws.

To say that Baptism of Desire is not true is to accuse the Catholic Church for allowing error to be taught in her catechisms and practiced in her laws, and permitting it to be taught as de fide, which St. Alphonsus Liguori (to name a few) stated that it was. SEE OBJECTION 4

You will firmly abide by the true decision of the Holy Roman Church and to this Holy See, which does not permit errors. (Lateran Council V, Bull *'Cum postquam'* by Pope Leo X)

To call Baptism of Desire and Blood a heresy is to say the Church issued a harmful law since it would be harmful to hold to a heresy, and the official law of the Church promotes it. SEE APPENDIX 4

This one argument alone ends the debate.

Canon 737 declares, *"Baptism, the gateway and foundation of the Sacraments, actually or at least in desire is necessary for all for salvation...."*

This canon ends the debate on the Church's official interpretation of Canon 4 of the Council of Trent.

These two canon laws are not just part of the Western Church. They are also understood and practiced in the East, which means these are universal Church laws in two senses.

The consequences of rejecting the law of the Church is damning because the application of the law trickles down to the practice of the Church. We have funeral masses for catechumes. Those who reject BOD would have to say that these masses lead to impiety because they imply Baptism of Desire and would necessarily lead one to believe in Baptism of Desire.

If anyone says that the ceremonies, vestments, and outward signs, which the Catholic Church uses in the celebration of Masses, are incentives to impiety rather than the services of piety: let him be anathema [cf. n. 943]. Can. 7. The Council of Trent, Session XXII, (D. 954).

Those against BOD would necessarily reject funeral masses for catechumens.

If anyone shall say that the received and approved rites of the Catholic Church accustomed to be used in the solemn administration of the sacraments may be disdained or omitted by the minister without sin and at pleasure, or may be changed by any pastor of the churches to other new ones: let him be anathema. Can. 13. The Council of Trent, Session VII, (D. 856).

Those against BOD would necessarily be required to have the priest disdain the approved rite of funeral masses said for catechumens.

Pay close attention.

Can. 1204: Ecclesiastical burial consists in bringing the body to the church, **holding the funeral service over the same in the church,** and entombing it in a place destined for the burial of departed Catholics.

Funeral services may include masses when priests are present. However, according to Can. 1241: For those who have been deprived of ecclesiastical burial no [public] Requiem Mass, no anniversary, or other public funeral service may be held.

Now notice the words in Can. 1239. It is speaking about *ecclesiastical* burial, not just any burial. Now Catechumens are to be given an ecclesiastical burial and treated as baptized, which means they may receive funeral masses. Read an official commentary from 1918 below...

Can. 1239 § 1. Ad sepukuram ccclcsiasticam non sunt admit;-* tendi qui sine baptismo decesserint. § 2. Catechumeni qui nulla sua culpa sine baptismo moriantur, baptizatis accensendi sunt. § 3. Omnes baptizati sepultura ecclesiastica do- nandi sunt, nisi eadem a iure expressc priventur.

I. Baptism, being the Sacrament of initiation and sign of communion with the Church and membership in the same, is the fundamental condition of receiving a. Catholic burial. Baptism may be received by desire — • baptismus flaminis — and this is generally supposed in,
those who had received instructions in the faith (catechumens). Hence our canon in its first section states that no person who has died -without Baptism may be admitted to ecclesiastical burial. This includes even unbaptized infants, though it is generally admitted that a child not yet born may be buried together with the mother in consecrated ground. 1 Besides, it appears, at least to many, very awkward and offensive if this law should be applied to burial in the ancestral grave. Yet, unless non-compliance must be tolerated in order to avoid greater evils, the law should be enforced. 2

§ 2. Catechumens, or such as are preparing to embrace the Catholic faith, **may be given ecclesiastical burial.** if they have died without baptism through no fault of their own. For they are to be compared to baptized persons. 3 Thus if a would-be convert would die suddenly, with no priest at hand, as may happen in places which missionaries seldom visit, he could receive ecclesiastical burial. (Professor of Canon Law, Rev. P. Charles Augustine, O.S.B., D.D.)

The Practice of the Church

Every year for over 1600 years, the traditional Breviary commemorates St. Emerantiana, virgin and martyr, who died with the Baptism of Blood. SEE OBJECTION 31

The Breviary states:

"Emerantiana, a Roman virgin, step-sister of the blessed Agnes, while still a catechumen, burning with faith and charity, when she vehemently rebuked idol-worshippers who were stealing from Christians, was stoned and struck down by the crowd which she had angered. Praying in her agony at the tomb of holy Agnes, baptized by her own blood which she poured forth unflinchingly for Christ, she gave up her soul to God."

This virgin and martyr died in Rome about the year 350. A church was built over her grave. According to the Catholic Encyclopedia (1908), some days after the death of St. Agnes, Emerentiana who was still a catechumen, went to the grave to pray, and while praying she was suddenly attacked by the pagans and killed with stones. Her feast is kept on January 23 and she is again commemorated on Sept 16 under the phrase in *caemeterio maiore* (where she is buried). She is represented in the iconography of the church with stones in her lap and a palm of lily in her hands.

The Catholic Church states in her liturgy that she was *"baptized in her own blood."*

To say Baptism of Blood is heretical, is to say the discipline of the church is harmful since the liturgy proclaims it. However, the Church has solemnly stated that She cannot issue a harmful discipline or law as has been already noted.

To deny Emerentiana was baptized by blood is ridiculous and has no merit unless one is bent on denying the universal doctrine. It also would mean the Church is in error in officially acknowledging her as a martyr who was baptized in her own blood.

The liturgy has some more instances:

In the Breviary in the office of Nov. 10, is that of St. Respicius.

"During the reign of the emperor Decius, as Tryphon was preaching the faith of Jesus Christ and striving to persuade all men to worship the Lord, he was arrested by the henchmen of Decius. First, he was tortured on the rack, his flesh torn with iron hooks, then hung head downward, his feet pierced with red hot nails. He was beaten by clubs, scorched by burning torches held against his body. As a result of seeing him endure all these tortures so courageously, the tribune Respicius was converted to the faith of Christ the Lord. Upon the spot he publicly declared himself to be a Christian. Respicius was then tortured in various ways, and together with Tryphon, dragged to a statue of Jupiter. As Tryphon prayed, the statue fell down. After this occurred both were mercilessly beaten with leaden tipped whips and thus attained to glorious martyrdom."

St. Victor of Braga of Portugal is a saint who is commemorated in the Breviary on April 11. During the reign of Diocletian, he refused to adore an idol and with great courage confessed his belief in Jesus Christ. He was severely tortured and then decapitated being baptized in his own blood.

The Teaching of Popes

Pope Innocent II who reigned from 1130-1143. He wrote to the Bishop of Cremona in a letter entitled *Apostolicam Sedem:*

"We assert without hesitation (on the authority of the holy Fathers Augustine and Ambrose) that the 'priest' whom you indicated (in your letter) had died without the water of baptism, because he persevered in the Faith of Holy Mother Church and in the confession of the name of Christ, was freed from original sin and attained the joys of the heavenly fatherland. Read [brother] in the eighth book of Augustine's City of God where among other things it is written: 'Baptism is administered invisibly to one whom not contempt of religion, but death excludes.' Read again the book also of the blessed Ambrose concerning the death of Valentinian where he says the same thing. Therefore, to questions concerning the dead, you should hold the opinions of the learned Fathers, and in your church you should join in prayers and you should have sacrifices offered to God for the 'priest' mentioned." SEE OBJECTION 22

Pope Innocent III: letter to a Bishop Berthold of Metz on August 28, 1206:

"You have, to be sure, intimated that a certain Jew, when at the point of death, since he lived only among Jews, immersed himself in water while saying: 'I baptize myself in the name of the Father, and of the Son, and of the Holy Spirit, Amen.'

"We respond that, since there should be a distinction between the one baptizing and the one baptized, as is clearly gathered from the words of the Lord, when he says to the Apostles: 'Go baptize all nations in the names etc.' (cf. Matt. 28:19, the Jew mentioned must be baptized again by another, that it may be shown that he who is baptized is one person, and he who baptizes another... If, however, such a one had died immediately, he would have rushed to his heavenly home without delay because of the faith of the sacrament, although not because of the sacrament of faith." SEE OBJECTION 23

Pope Pius IX wrote in *Singulari Quidem*, On the Church in Austria Encyclical, March 17, 1856:

[17] Outside of the Church, nobody can hope for life or salvation unless he is excused through ignorance beyond his control. SEE OBJECTION 24

Pope Pius IX wrote in *Quanto Conficiamur Moerore*, On Promotion of False Doctrines Encyclical, August 10, 1863:

7. Here, too, our beloved sons and venerable brothers, it is again necessary to mention and censure a very grave error entrapping some Catholics who believe that it is possible to arrive at eternal salvation although living in error and alienated from the true faith and Catholic unity. Such belief is certainly opposed to Catholic teaching. There are, of course, those who are struggling with invincible ignorance about our most holy religion. Sincerely observing the natural law and its precepts inscribed by God on all hearts and ready to obey God, they live honest lives and are able to attain eternal life by the efficacious virtue of divine light and grace. Because God knows, searches and clearly understands the minds, hearts, thoughts, and nature of all, his supreme kindness and clemency do not permit anyone at all who is not guilty of deliberate sin to suffer eternal punishments.

8. Also well known is the Catholic teaching that no one can be saved outside the Catholic Church. Eternal salvation cannot be obtained by those who oppose the authority and statements of the same Church and are stubbornly separated from the unity of the Church and also from the successor of Peter, the Roman Pontiff, to whom "the custody of the vineyard has been committed by the Savior."[4] The words of Christ are clear enough: "If he refuses to listen even to the Church, let him be to you a Gentile and a tax collector;"[5] "He who hears you hears me, and he who rejects you, rejects me, and he who rejects me, rejects him who sent me;"[6] "He who does not believe will be condemned;"[7] "He who does not believe is already condemned;"[8] "He who is not with me is against me, and he who does not gather with me scatters."[9] The Apostle Paul says that such persons are "perverted and self-condemned;"[10] the Prince of the Apostles calls them "false teachers . . . who will

secretly bring in destructive heresies, even denying the Master. . . bringing upon themselves swift destruction."[11] SEE OBJECTION 25

Catechism of St. Pius X written and promulgated 18 October 1912 by **Pope St. Pius X**:

**LETTER OF HIS HOLINESS POPE PIUS X
TO CARDINAL PETER RESPIGHI,
VICAR OF ROME,
WHICH IS APPROVED BY
THE CATECHISM OF CHRISTIAN DOCTRINE
FOR THE DIOCESE AND THE ECCLESIASTICAL PROVINCE
OF ROME**

29 Q: But if a man through no fault of his own is outside the Church, can he be saved?

A: If he is outside the Church through no fault of his, that is, if he is in good faith, and if he has received Baptism, or at least has the implicit desire of Baptism; and if, moreover, he sincerely seeks the truth and does God's will as best he can such a man is indeed separated from the body of the Church, but is united to the soul of the Church and consequently is on the way of salvation. SEE OBJECTION 26

The following is an interesting piece of tidbit not used to defend Baptism of Desire and Blood (at least I'm not aware of any).

Pope Benedict XV Encyclical, *In Praeclara Summorum*, On Dante promulgated on April 30, 1921 encourages the faithful to read Dante.

In it the Pope states:

Among the many celebrated geniuses of whom the Catholic faith can boast who have left undying fruits in literature and art especially, besides other fields of learning, and to whom civilization and religion are ever in debt, highest stands the name of Dante Alighieri…

to show even more clearly than before the intimate union of Dante with this Chair of Peter, and how the praises showered on that distinguished name necessarily redound in no small measure to the honour of the Catholic Church...

And first of all, inasmuch as the divine poet throughout his whole life professed in exemplary manner the Catholic religion...

Indeed, his Commedia, which deservedly earned the title of Divina, while it uses various symbolic images and records the lives of mortals on earth, has for its true aim the glorification of the justice and providence of God who rules the world through time and all eternity and punishes and rewards the actions of individuals and human society. It is thus that, according to the Divine Revelation, in this poem shines out the majesty of God One and Three, the Redemption of the human race operated by the Word of God made Man, the supreme loving-kindness and charity of Mary, Virgin and Mother, Queen of Heaven, and lastly the glory on high of Angels, Saints and men; then the terrible contrast to this, the pains of the impious in Hell; then the middle world, so to speak, between Heaven and Hell, Purgatory, the Ladder of souls destined after expiation to supreme beatitude...

Therefore the divine poet depicted the triple life of souls as he imagined it in a such way as to illuminate with the light of the true doctrine of the faith the condemnation of the impious, the purgation of the good spirits and the eternal happiness of the blessed before the final judgment. 5. But among the truths that shine out in the triple poem of Alighieri as in his other works We think that these things may serve as teaching for men of our times...

Thus, as he based the whole structure of his poem on these sound religious principles, no wonder that we find in it a treasure of Catholic teaching; not only, that is, essence of Christian philosophy and theology, but the compendium of the divine laws which should govern the constitution and administration of States; for Dante Alighieri was not a man to maintain, for the purpose of giving greater glory to country or pleasure to ruler, that the State may neglect justice and right which he knew well to be the main foundation of civil nations...

And you, beloved children, whose lot it is to promote learning under the magisterium of the Church, continue as you are doing to love and tend the noble poet whom We do not hesitate to call the most eloquent singer of the Christian idea. The more profit you draw from study of him the higher will be your culture, irradiated by the splendours of truth, and the stronger and more spontaneous your devotion to the Catholic Faith.

This is important because Dante wrote, in his Divine Comedy, about souls who were not in the Catholic Church but were found in Purgatory.

Purgatory is where saved souls go to be purged of all impurities before entering Heaven. How could Dante have in Purgatory those who were not living inside the Church unless Baptism of Desire or Blood were involved?

If Baptism of Desire is heretical, then we have Pope Benedict XV actually promoting the heresy because the pope says Dante's work *"depicted the triple life of souls as he imagined it in a such way as to illuminate with the light of the true doctrine of the faith,"* and that *"he based the whole structure of his poem on these sound religious principles, no wonder that we find in it a treasure of Catholic teaching."*

Not only does Benedict promote it, but says it is the true doctrine of the faith. This is an astonishing fact that proves the Church indeed holds the doctrine as the truth.

The 1949 Letter

Many BOD defenders use the 1949 letter from the Holy Office to refute those who object to Baptism of Desire.

On August 8, 1949, Cardinal Marchetti-Selvaggiani of the Headquarters of the Holy Office issued a letter to Archbishop Richard Cushing of Boston that attempted to condemned Father Leonard Feeney and the position he defended. This letter is used in seminaries and universities all across America.

The 1949 letter was never placed in the Acta Apostolicae Sedis, which is the publication where all official acts of the Church are registered. Without this registration, the letter simply does not exist officially in the Church. (In 1963, the letter was placed in *Enchiridion Symbolorum* known as Denzinger. The editor of Denzinger was Rev. Karl Rahner, one of the most liberal and influential theologians in his time. Rev. Rahner pulled the letter from the non-authoritative source of The American Ecclesiastical Review of October 1952.)

A month after the 1949 letter was initially sent to Boston, Fr. Feeney responded in a letter back to Cardinal Marchetti-Selvaggiani of the Holy Office stating, *"It is now being proclaimed everywhere in American newspapers, both secular and Catholic, that the Holy Office edited an official decree, signed by you, and approved by you, and approved by the Roman Pontiff, and partially quoted by the official newspaper of the diocese of Boston, The Pilot, in which decree it is announced that the dogma of the Church 'Outside the Church there is no salvation' we must now interpret according to the norms of American liberalism according to which salvation is bestowed on everyone on account of his own sincerity."*

The Cardinal never replied.

The question remains whether the Pope actually approved of the contents of the 1949 letter as it was finally stated. However, 11 months after Fr. Feeney's response back to Rome, Pope Pius XII issued another encyclical *Humani Generis* in 1950 stating, *"Some say they are not bound by the doctrine, explained in Our Encyclical Letter of a few years ago, and based on the sources of revelation, which teaches that the Mystical Body of Christ and the Roman Catholic Church are one and the same thing. Some reduce to a meaningless formula the necessity of belonging to the true Church in order to gain eternal salvation...These and like errors, it is clear, have crept in among certain of Our sons who are deceived by imprudent zeal for souls or by false science. To them We are compelled with grief to repeat once again truths already well known, and to point out with solicitude clear errors and dangers of error."*

Fr. Feeney saw this encyclical as a sign that the Holy Father was on his side.

Fr. Feeney did recognize that man could be justified apart from the Sacrament of Baptism but could not enter Heaven without it. This is indeed incorrect and is addressed in Objection number 32.

The 1949 should not be used to defend Baptism of Desire at all. It is very poorly written and does not teach Baptism of Desire correctly.

IN SUMMARY

1. Invincible ignorance does not save, nor does it help in salvation in anyway. It is the severest handicap to salvation.

2. Salvation does not ever come in, through, or by any other religion except the Catholic Faith. There are no exceptions whatsoever to the dogma, 'Outside the Catholic Church There Is No Salvation,' even under extraordinary conditions.

3. The Catholic Faith and the Sacrament of Baptism are the necessary means that one enters into the Catholic Church.

4. Baptism of Desire is the doctrine taught by the Catholic Church that it is possible to be saved apart from the Sacrament of Baptism only under extraordinary conditions.

5. Only those who can be saved by Baptism of Desire are those above the age of reason who live honest lives, open to God's grace, and are perfectly contrite in the sorrow for their sins, and are infused the Catholic Faith immediately before or at death.

6. Baptism of Desire is a miracle performed by God.

7. Un-baptized infants cannot be saved by Baptism of Desire.

8. Baptism of Blood is the doctrine taught by the Catholic Church that one who without the Sacrament of Baptism sheds his blood for Christ wanting to be united to Christ through the Catholic Church will be saved. There are Catholic Saints who have died in this way.

9. Un-baptized infants can be saved by Baptism of Blood.

10. Those who knowingly object to Baptism of Desire and/or Blood are not Catholics.

The Objections to Baptism of Desire and Blood

> **Objection 1:** The Doctrine goes against Christ's Words in John 3:5. Each time we see the Church teaching the necessity of the Sacrament of Water Baptism, it understands John 3:5 "as it is written."

This would mean that Pope St. Pius V who promulgated a Catechism that teaches it and St. Charles Borromeo for its editing were against Our Lord. It means St. Alphonsus Liquori and Pope St. Pius X are rejecting Christ's words for teaching BOD as de fide. It means that many great Popes, Saints and ten other Doctors of the Church are against what Our Lord said *"as it is written,"* but this is absurd.

According to the Church, the *"Unless…Cannot"* in John 3:5, is not absolute under all conditions. The Sacrament falls under the ordinary means in ordinary cases. BOD falls under the extraordinary means in extraordinary cases.

The extraordinary means does not apply to all of the sacraments.

One cannot change bread and wine into Christ's Body and Blood by faith and desire, nor can one be ordained by faith and desire. But one can be justified by faith and desire at death provided that the Sacrament of Baptism is not made available. Even then, it is God who granted one the Faith and desire for it, and it would be pretty worthless to grant one the Faith along with desire with perfect contrition and then send him off to hell. God is just and He doesn't waste.

> **Objection 2:** Pope Paul III, Council of Trent, Session 6, Chap. 11 on Justification: *"…no one should make use of that rash statement forbidden under anathema by the Fathers, that the commandments of God are impossible to observe for a man who is justified. 'FOR GOD DOES NOT COMMAND IMPOSSIBILITIES, but by commanding*

> admonishes you both to do what you can do, and to pray for what you cannot do..."
>
> The Council of Trent teaches: *"Christ cannot command impossibilities"*, therefore, since God commands to be Baptized by water, water will always be made possible for men of goodwill.

First, notice the context. Trent's statement is speaking about, *"a man who is justified"* obeying the commandments of God. It's addressing those who would argue that, *"the just man sins at least venially in every good work [can. 25], (what is more intolerable) that he merits eternal punishments; and that they also who declare that the just sin in all works, if in those works, in order to stimulate their own sloth and to encourage themselves to run in the race, with this (in view), that above all God may be glorified, they have in view also the eternal reward [can. 26, 31], since it is written: 'I have inclined my heart to do thy justifications on account of the reward' [Ps. 118:112], and of Moses the Apostle says, that he "looked to the reward" [Heb. 11:26]."* (Trent, Session 6, Ch. 11)

For the sake of the argument, let's presume that the phrase applied to the sacrament of Baptism. Since Christ cannot command impossibilities, if the Sacrament of Baptism is made impossible, then Christ's command to be baptized by water wouldn't apply, thus faith, desire, and contrition suffices.

Not only does Trent's statement not contradict Baptism of Desire, but rather, it supports it.

Baptism of Desire works just fine with the teaching.

The command to be baptized by water is the command of invitation. Christ invites us to eternal life.

For example, the Calvinists know the quotes of Our Lord to *"come all who labor...and I will give you rest."* For the Calvinists, Christ doesn't really mean it. The Calvinist doctrine is Christ gives only the elect the desire and power to come and they can't refuse because they believe God's grace to come is irresistible. Therefore, Christ does not give everyone the desire and power to come or else every single person will come and be saved. The Calvinists believe Christ commands impossibilities.

Christ commands us to come to Him and be saved. If God must absolutely command water and another person (to perform the Sacrament) for one to be saved, then He would have to absolutely make them available. This would necessarily limit the power of God, since it would take His own creation to fulfill what would necessarily be lacking in His power to do it without them. This is illogical especially if you're the only believer around.

God's power is way beyond His creation. In other words, the sacraments don't limit His power for He is all-powerful and always has been.

Therefore, it is not in the Baptism itself that God commands. It is in the Baptism of water **to be saved.** SEE OBJECTION 23

Baptism is a sacrament that gives man the means to Heaven, not an obstacle.

We need food to survive and live and God must provide it for us or we will die. Like Baptism, God must provide us with the desire, the faith, the water, and the person to perform it or else we can't enter Heaven.

God could if He so willed keep us alive without food. He is not absolutely dependent upon His creation *"food"* to keep us alive. As a matter of fact, we have had saints who lived over 25 years without food but on the Eucharist alone, such as St. Nicholas of Flue (1417-1487). The saints wouldn't even need the Holy Sacrament if God so willed it.

Food is the necessary means to live, but God could provide a way without it in extraordinary cases.

Baptism is the necessary means for salvation, but God could provide a way without it in extraordinary cases.

Of course, it would be a miracle, but that only proves it is possible. BOD is the teaching that it is possible for God to save without the Sacrament of Baptism. It would take a miracle for sure, but miracles happen every day. The Consecration of Bread and Wine into the Body and Blood of Christ is a daily miracle.

If one wanted to argue that God could do it but wouldn't, he would be arguing against God's love, mercy, and justice.

Interesting, God does actually perform extraordinary miracles such as raising the dead for the very purpose of Baptism. This proves that he could save others without Baptism. If God raised some from physical death by the power of His Holy Name alone, then He could save others from spiritual death by the power of His Holy Name alone.

Objection 3: What about the great miracles of miraculous springs for catechumens to be Baptized on their way to be executed, and raisings of the dead for the purpose of receiving the water baptisms, and the bilocation of missionaries to spread the Gospel? The bilocations prove that God will even miraculously send a missionary for Baptism. Why have these miracles but to demonstrate the necessity of water baptism? Some of the great miracles actually state that the miracle was performed precisely because Baptism was needed. If BOD is possible, then the miracle would not be needed to be performed. SEE APPENDIX 7

The answer is simple. God is stressing the importance and necessity of the Sacrament of Baptism, not to deny the doctrine of Baptism of Desire. Besides, Baptism of Desire requires perfect contrition. The Sacrament assures salvation where as Baptism of Desire or Blood makes for a possibility only provided all the necessary requirements are also present.

The possible answer for the miracles that were performed just so that Baptism can be done comes from simple reasoning.

Let's take a look at the miracle of St. Patrick:

In the country of Neyll, a King Echu allowed St. Patrick to receive his beloved daughter Cynnia as a nun, though he bewailed the fact that his royal line would thereby end without issue. The king exacted a promise from Patrick not to insist that he be baptized, yet to promise him the heavenly kingdom. Patrick agreed, and left the matter in the hands of God.

Sometime later King Echu lay dying. He sent a messenger to St. Patrick to tell him he desired Baptism and the heavenly kingdom. To those around him the King gave an order that he not be buried until Patrick came. Patrick, then in the monastery of Saballum, two days' journey away, knew of the situation through the Holy Spirit before the messenger even arrived. He left to go to the King, but arrived to find Echu dead.

St. Patrick revived the King, instructed him, and baptized him. He asked Echu to relate what he had seen of the joys of the just and the pains of the wicked, so that his account could be used for the proving of Patrick's preaching. Echu told of many other-world wonders and of how, in the heavenly country, he had seen the place that Patrick promised him. But the King could not enter in because he was unbaptized.

Then St. Patrick asked Echu if he would rather live longer in this world, or go to the place prepared for him in the heavenly kingdom. The King answered that all the world had was emptiest smoke compared to the celestial joys. Then having received the Eucharist, he fell asleep in the Lord. (Taken from *Raised from the Dead* by TAN Books.)

It would seem the miracle was primarily the resurrection of the dead King to prove to Ireland's pagans of the one True God, not necessarily for the benefit of King Echu. King Echu probably died without perfect contrition, because he had to be instructed in the Faith after Patrick resurrected him. This means he procrastinated with Patrick about being a Christian. However, in God's mercy, was given another chance because he pleased God for being open to His grace. Therefore, three things were accomplished in this miracle. It made the power of God manifest in this great miracle of resurrection from the dead, and the mercy of God to save a man who pleased Him but not enough to enter Heaven apart from the Sacrament, and lastly, to tell what was on the other side, and why one should not procrastinate but get instructed in the Faith so he can be Baptized. It was a warning and a lesson to all.

This miracle of resurrection from the dead proves that God can save without Baptism, not prove Baptism is absolutely necessary under all conditions. After all, if St. Patrick (in the name of Jesus) raised the King from the dead, then God could raise men from spiritual death without the Sacraments.

When Jesus asked, the crowd after forgiving the lame man to get up and walk, *"Which is easier, to say, `Your sins are forgiven you,' or to say, `Rise and walk?"* (Luke 5:23)

Christ proved that he could forgive the sins or spiritually save the lame man by the miracle of the physical healing of the man.

All the miracle stories for the Sacrament of Baptism are like this historical and Biblical story.

God performs miracles so that those who need Baptism receive it. This proves that God can perform the miracle of saving other men apart from Baptism.

There have been other reports of those who lived as Protestants who made it to Purgatory. We can read about them in *"Conversations Between a Nun and a Soul in Purgatory from Nov. 1873 to Nov 1890"* printed by Lapanto Press, and *"Purgatory Explained by the Lives and Legends of the Saints"* by Fr F.X. Shouppe, S.J printed by Tan Books.

If these stories are true, then it would mean that BOD is true. The Sacrament of Baptism does Protestants no good without the true Faith. Therefore, God must infuse them the Faith immediately before or at death. It could be argued that they were baptized and Baptism of Desire wouldn't apply. However, BOD is the teaching that God brings those who lived outside the Church into the Church. Remember, Baptism of Desire is just a designated term for this teaching.

Baptism may not be valid in most Protestant churches anyway since most of them don't baptize with the intent of the Catholic Church, which is to forgive sins. This is why the mere desire for Baptism is not good enough.

> **Objection 4:** St. Alphonsus Liquori stated: *"Now it is de fide that men are also saved by Baptism of desire, by virtue of the Canon Apostolicam, "de presbytero non baptizato" and of the Council of Trent, session 6, Chapter 4 where it is said that no one can be saved "without the laver of regeneration or the desire for it".* Moral Theology, Bk. 6, nn. 95-7. Concerning Baptism
>
> St. Robert Bellarmine also said geocentrism is de fide but Pope Benedict XV in *Praeclara Summorum* (#4), April 20,1921, implied that it was not. Since St. Bellarmine's opinion was wrong on geocentrism, St. Alphonsus's opinion on Baptism of Desire being de fide is also wrong.

The problem with this argument is St. Robert Bellarmine is not stating a heresy is de fide. Geocentrism and heliocentrism are scientific theories. St. Bellarmine was referring to Scripture on the movement of the earth and merely saying Scripture cannot be in error. No heresy is involved here, but rather only a misunderstanding as to what infallibility entails. Since the First Vatican Council, we know now in certainty that science is not part of it and St. Bellarmine lived before then.

However, if Baptism of Desire is heresy, then you have St. Alphonsus Liguori saying a heresy is dogma.

This argument is comparing apples with oranges. It simply does not apply, but it goes much further than that.

For those who say BOD/BOB is heretical and that it cannot be held as a Catholic would say St. Alphonsus Liquori is a heretic, since he lived after all the dogmatic teachings. He would necessarily have to be considered a formal heretic since he was not ignorant of the facts.

> **Objection 5:** Pope St. Siricius and his Letter to Himerius in 385:
>
> *"As we maintain that the observance of the holy Paschal time should in no way be relaxed, in the same way we desire that infants who, on account of their age, cannot yet speak, or those who, in any necessity, are in want of* **the water** *of holy baptism, be succored with all possible speed, for fear that,* **if those who leave this world should be deprived of the life of the Kingdom for having been refused the source of salvation which they desired,** *this may lead to the ruin of our souls.* **If those threatened with shipwreck, or the attack of enemies, or the uncertainties of a siege, or those put in a hopeless condition due to some bodily sickness, ask for what in their faith is their only help, let them receive at the very moment of their request the reward of regeneration they beg for. Enough of past mistakes!** *From now on, let all the priests observe the aforesaid rule if they do not want to be separated from the solid apostolic rock on which Christ has built his universal Church."* Fr. Jacques Dupuis, S.J. and Fr. Josef Neuner, S.J., The Christian Faith, Sixth Revised and Enlarged Edition, Staten Island, NY: Alba House, 1996, p. 540.
>
> This pope is saying desire for baptism does not save.

The first problem is those who use this argument usually reject other papal statements (such as Pope Pius IX, *Singulari Quidem* 1856 or Pope Innocent III, *Debitumpastoralis officii*, August 28, 1206 to name a few) that clearly speak or imply the doctrine of Baptism of Desire by referring to them as mere letters where infallibility is void. Yet, this very quote is a letter only. This shows their hypocrisy.

Anyway, does this quote by Pope Siricius deny the doctrine of Baptism of Desire or refute through implication that it is impossible to be saved by Baptism of Desire? Of course not.

Those who by necessity desiring water Baptism may very well be lost because Baptism of Desire is not accomplished by merely desiring it. As a matter of fact, there is always the fear that those who die without the Sacrament of Baptism, may be lost because we do not know for sure if they had perfect contrition along with their desiring and faith.

Pope Siricius says delaying such infants or men *"may lead to the ruin of our souls."* In other words, it would be a sin to delay them.

The second part of the quotation reiterates the first part. Perfect contrition may not be in their faith, and Baptism is their only help to bring them to salvation.

The Roman Catechism states, *"In Case of Necessity Adults May be Baptized at Once."* (p 180)

Why does the Catechism say this if it just stated 3 paragraphs earlier "should any foreseen accident make it impossible for adults to be washed in the salutary waters, their intention and determination to receive Baptism and their repentance for past sins, will avail them to grace and righteousness?"

Is the Roman Catechism contradicting itself? Of course not. The doctrine of Baptism of Desire requires repentance of sins (which of course must fall under perfect contrition), faith, and desire. The Sacrament of Baptism does not require perfect contrition.

Pope Siricius is saying the same thing as the Roman Catechism.

Objection 6: Another interpretation can be given for the following Canon 4 of Trent: *"that although all are not necessary for every individual, without them or without the desire of them,"* and Decree on Justification - (Session 6, Chapter 4): *"except through the laver of regeneration or a desire for it."*

This does not imply Baptism of Desire. It simply is distinguishing all that is necessary for the un-baptized – Laver of Regeneration, for infants and adults, or a desire for it – adults only. If Trent had said, "...laver of regeneration 'and' a desire for it," then it would have invalidated all infant baptisms. Had Trent merely stated, "laver of regeneration" without mentioning a desire for, then it would not be adequate since desire is necessary for adults. So Trent does not say that the laver of regeneration can effect justification, nor does it say that the desire for Baptism can effect justification. It is simply telling

> us what cannot be missing in infants, and what cannot be missing in adults. Period!
>
> Canon 4 should be interpreted in light of and after Canon 2 which states, *"if anyone shall say that real and natural water is not necessary for baptism, and on that account those words of Our Lord Jesus Christ: 'Unless a man be born again of water and the Holy Spirit' (John 3:5), are distorted into some sort of metaphor: Let him be anathema."*
>
> Christ is clear about the water. He didn't say unless a man is baptized he cannot enter eternal life, but says water. And Scripture also says that there is one Lord, one Faith, and one Baptism, not 3 baptisms.
>
> Canon 5 states: *"If anyone says that baptism is optional, that is, not necessary for salvation, let him be anathema."*

    This argument for the Council of Trent is interesting for it is another interpretation that would appear on the surface to fit the position of those who oppose Baptism of Desire.

    The problem with this interpretation is one would have to go to an English professor to see if this interpretation could be rendered in this fashion. Why is this problematic?

    Ambiguous statements are to be rendered heretical according to Pope Pius VI in *Auctorem Fidei* telling us how heretics operate through their ambiguous teachings.

    The Council of Trent would have to be rendered heretical for its ambiguous statements on the laver of regeneration. Since it was so ambiguous, one would have to go search out a professor to figure out how Trent is to be understood by the Faithful. After all, since the normal way of interpreting Trent, indeed the only way anybody has ever interpreted it, even by its own Catechism issued by Rome, until recently by those who object to BOD is that understanding of Baptism of Desire as we know it.

    Another point is desire is not all that is needed by adults. Faith is what is needed and this objection does not follow logic. If Trent were telling what must not be missing for adults, *"without Faith"* would have been the words not *"without the desire of them."* As been noted in Objection 3, Baptism in most Protestant churches is invalid because the intent of the Catholic Church is missing, which is to forgive sins. This is why the mere desire for Baptism is not good enough making this argument out of Trent ridiculous.

BOD/BOB does not distort Canon 2 into some kind of metaphor. This Canon is referring to those who say that it is not Baptism of water at all that Christ was speaking about. It was going against the Protestant heresies that denied the Catholic Teaching of Water Baptism. Some Protestants say the water, which Christ referred to, was a metaphorical expression being washed in the word of God. Baptism is a work needed for salvation and Protestants reject works as necessary for salvation. This is what Trent was condemning in Canon 2.

As for Canon 5, Baptism of Water is not optional. One cannot opt out of it and be saved. BOD/BOB are for those who weren't given an option.

> **Objection 7:** The Council of Trent on the sacraments: Canon IV.
>
> *"If anyone saith that the sacraments of the New Law are not necessary unto salvation, but superfluous; and that without them, or without the desire thereof men obtain of God through faith alone the grace of justification; though all (the sacraments) are not indeed necessary for every individual; let him be anathema."*
>
> Following the logic of BOD, is this not saying that all of the sacraments can be received by desire? The original Latin says the same.

This argument misconstrues what Trent was saying on the *"desire thereof."* Canon IV obviously was not meaning the *"desire thereof"* to apply to all of the sacraments such as Holy Orders for it only addressed the desire on the part of Baptism in session 6. The rendering of *"or"* to mean *"and"* makes no difference at all. Water Baptism already presumes a desire for it in adults and to have to say *"or desire thereof"* would be superfluous. However, the context as understood by the Faith renders it this way, *"You cannot enter heaven without water (baptism) or 'at least' a desire for it."*

It is also presumed that the desire includes faith, perfect contrition, and the impossibility of the water. We understand this by reading all that the Church has said on the issue of justification. This is how the Church understands Her own Doctrine. Anything else is a mere Protestant personal interpretation, which goes against the Magisterium. It is not a desire alone as the article says. This is just another straw-man argument.

Those who use arguments such as this accuse the BOD believers of not liking what Trent means, but in reality, it is they who don't like what Trent means. They don't want to see it and therefore ignore the history of the Church or make up excuses.

> **Objection 8:** To say that there are *"three baptisms,"* as many unfortunately do, is heretical. There is only one baptism, which is celebrated in water (de fide).

Those who *"unfortunately"* do are the popes and saints of the Church. The bottom line is that there is only one baptism under ordinary conditions. There are two other *"so-called"* baptisms under extraordinary conditions.

> **Objection 9:** The law of the Church is not infallible and was never signed by the pope. It is erroneous.

This argument is saying the law is meaningless, has no authority, and in the end harmful. The problem is this law is the official law of the Church and is recognized by the popes even if they didn't write or sign them. Not only that, but you can never use the law to prove, to demonstrate, or use against someone in error. This is an illogical and foolish argument. However, the Church teaches that this universal Law is infallible. SEE APPENDIX 4

However, the 1917 Code of Canon Law was approved by the Church. It doesn't have to be signed by the pope. There was a big celebration by Pope Benedict XV when he promulgated the Code of

Law. Pope St. Pius X condemned those who don't accept the authority of those decisions that are approved by the Pontiff. The Code of Law has been approved by Pope Benedict XV and all those who reject it are condemned by Pope St. Pius X.

> **Objection 10:** Pope Eugene IV, Council of Florence, Sess. 8, Nov. 22, 1439, *ex cathedra*: composed by most blessed Athanasius, which is as follows:
>
> *"Whoever wishes to be saved, needs above all to hold the Catholic faith; unless each one preserves this whole and inviolate, he will without a doubt perish in eternity.– But the Catholic faith is this, that we worship one God in the Trinity, and the Trinity in unity; neither confounding the persons, nor dividing the substance; for there is one person of the Father, another of the Son, another of the Holy Spirit, their glory is equal, their majesty co-eternal...and in this Trinity there is nothing first or later, nothing greater or less, but all three persons are coeternal and coequal with one another, so that in every respect, as has already been said above, both unity in Trinity, and Trinity in unity must be worshipped. Therefore let him who wishes to be saved, think thus concerning the Trinity. "But it is necessary for eternal salvation that he faithfully believe also in the incarnation of our Lord Jesus Christ...the Son of God is God and man... This is the Catholic faith; unless each one believes this faithfully and firmly, he cannot be saved."*
>
> This creed, therefore, eliminates the theory of invincible ignorance (that one above the age of reason can be saved without knowing Christ or the true Faith) and further renders those who preach it unable to profess this creed with honesty. This destroys the implicit faith/desire explanation.

This is not true, because invincible ignorance does not imply that one does not wish to be saved. Invincible ignorance referring to the Catholic Faith, not in atheism, is the issue for BOD/BOB. An invincibly ignorant man can wish to be saved, and God can infuse the Catholic Faith in the man. God's power is not limited here. This objection is silly.

> **Objection 11**: Pope St. Leo the Great, dogmatic letter to Flavian, Council of Chalcedon, 451:
>
> *"Let him heed what the blessed apostle Peter preaches, that sanctification by the Spirit is effected by the sprinkling of Christ's blood (1 Pet. 1:2); and let him not skip over the same apostle's words, knowing that you have been redeemed from the empty way of life you inherited from your fathers, not with corruptible gold and silver but by the precious blood of Jesus Christ, as of a lamb without stain or spot (1 Pet. 1:18). Nor should he withstand the testimony of blessed John the apostle: and the blood of Jesus, the Son of God, purifies us from every sin (1 Jn. 1:7); and again, This is the victory which conquers the world, our faith. Who is there who conquers the world save one who believes that Jesus is the Son of God? It is He, Jesus Christ, who has come through water and blood, not in water only, but in water and blood. And because the Spirit is truth, it is the Spirit who testifies. For there are three who give testimony – Spirit and water and blood. And the three are one. (1 Jn. 5:4-8) In other words, the Spirit of sanctification and the Blood of redemption and the water of Baptism, these three are one and remain indivisible. None of them is separable from its link with the others. The reason is that it is by this faith that the Catholic Church lives and grows, by believing that neither the humanity is without true divinity nor the divinity without the true humanity."*

No doubt this is true and Baptism of Desire does not say otherwise. The three are inseparable.

This doesn't mean that BOD or BOB is somehow separating Water of Baptism from the other two. Pope St. Leo the Great is saying those three things give testimony to the true Faith, and it is true that you can't separate any of them for it is through these "that the Catholic Church lives and grows."

BOD or BOB doesn't have anything to do with the Church living and growing as it journeys through time, which is the Church Militant. Rather, BOD or BOB is the explanation for the extraordinary situations on how one might enter the Church Suffering (purgatory) or Church Triumphant (Heaven).

How is it that so many saints and doctors of the Church taught Baptism of Desire? Was it because they were unaware of this statement by Pope Leo and simply were in error but with good faith?

Even Rome apparently wasn't aware of it either when it issued the Roman Catechism or when it issued the 1917 Code of Law.

Do you see the absurdity? The application is what we are dealing with and how Our Lord will deal with a certain situation. BOD and BOB applies to the extraordinary conditions.

> **Objection 12:** Would anyone have predicted that God would destroy everyone on the face of the earth, except for the eight souls of Noah's family, by drowning them? Certainly, of the perhaps millions who died at that time, there would have been many who would have repented if given more time. But God did not give it to them. God therefore let souls perish who could have been saved. Hence would God damn someone who should be intercepted by death on the way to being baptized with water?

Sure, if the wrong intent, wrong faith, no contrition, etc. were present.

This objection presupposes that there was some person in Noah's day that would have the qualifications required for BOD today.

From the historical and spiritual standpoints, if such a case existed, there would be two possibilities. Either that person would have perished in the deluge but would have gone to the limbo of the just where Noah, Abraham, etc went when they died, or would have been miraculously transported inside the ark.

> **Objection 13:** How does BOD work? When does a BOD person enter into a state of grace? The first moment he has desire or some time later? Most respond to this question with only at death. Well who says that! Which saint, council pope ever said when BOD is 'activated' or takes place in a persons soul - for salvation. That is at which moment does the soul enter grace? The term, Baptism of

Desire, is not defined by any pope, therefore, it is not a doctrine needed to be held by the faithful. We are free to disagree.

The Church and precisely the Roman Catechism does not give the precise answers and that is another reason why Vatican I needed to give those precise answers under a formula. What we have so far is that some way, somehow, God can and will infuse the faith (provided desire is present with perfect contrition) to save the person outside the ordinary means which is Water Baptism.

In other words, it is possible only. This we must believe, that God can and will work outside the Sacrament if He desires it. That's all the Church is saying.

Page 356 of Fundamentals of Catholic Dogma, Ludwig Ott states that Baptism of Desire is sentential fidei proxima, which means *"regarded by theologians generally as a truth of Revelation, but which has not been finally promulgated as such by the Church."* (Ott p 9) The term *"sentential fidei proxima"* also means that the doctrine is not an object of free judgment. The judgment of the Church is clearly in favor of it or else Trent would not have mentioned it as it did. Just because it has not been formally defined does not mean it is not true. It also does not mean that it is just a free opinion of theologians. It has gone way past that point.

The word *"Baptism of Desire"* is not a defined term. You don't have to necessarily believe in the term but rather the substance by which we use the term.

For instance, the word *"pope or papacy"* was not a defined term nor was it even used in the earliest days of Christianity, but the office of the pope most certainly existed. Catholics had to obey the authority of Peter even if there had not yet been defined the office of Peter. The inferences are Peter being made chief shepherd by Christ, he was given the keys, etc. The office has always been a doctrine whether it was defined or not. The substance of Shepherd, holder of the keys, etc., are what the early Christians went on to believe in the office of Peter.

The Holy Trinity was not a theological term for hundreds of years but that doesn't mean any Catholic could have rightly disputed the doctrine of the Trinity. The substance is what we are after here. The substance of the theological term albeit not dogmatized term BOD has been universally taught, by way of law of the Church and the Catechism issued by Trent and promulgated by Pope St. Pius V. The only logical interpretation of Trent, speaking on the Laver of Regeneration, and/or the *"desire for it"* by way of context, is BOD and not anything else.

> **Objection 14:** Implicit desire would imply Protestants, Muslims, Jews, pagans, etc could be saved in their religion because this desire denotes, *"What would they do if..."* Therefore, BOD is reduced down to an absurd principle.

The Church has not taught that anyone can reject Christ or the Church and be saved. Period. Pope Pius IX is the only pope to ever give the idea of implicit desire and he didn't say that one could reject Christ or the Church in his implicit desire. St. Justin Martyr and St. Robert Bellarmine were two saints famous for the implicit desire approach, but not in the sense that one could knowingly reject Christ in the process.

Some BOD believers will say to those who reject Christ and/or the Church can be saved by the *"What would you do if..."* This is not correct. Nobody would reject Christ and the Church if they knew what God had in store for them in Heaven. Even the Devil would have remained faithful. As a matter of fact, Christ even mentions Sodom would have not fallen if they had seen the mighty works of Christ (Matt 11:23), which would imply that Sodom would fit into the category of those *"What would you do if..."* and yet they fell.

Ignorance of the Faith will always damn the soul if God doesn't step in and infuse the Faith for reasons only He knows.

The following statements truly confirm this from some Fathers who perhaps didn't consider the possibility of implicit faith.

St. John Chrysostom said, *"We should mourn for those who are dying without the faith...and well should the pagan weep and lament* who, not knowing God, goes straight to punishment when he dies. Well should the Jew mourn who, not believing in Christ, has assigned his soul to perdition." (The *Sunday Sermons of the Great Fathers*, by M. F. Toal, Thomas, M. F.)

St. Augustine said, *"Every sinner is inexcusable, be he a sinner by original guilt or by an additional guilt of his own, whether he knows it or not, whether he judges it or not; for ignorance itself in those who do not want to know is without doubt a sin, and in those who are unable to know it is the penalty of sin. In neither case, then, is there a just excuse; but in both cases there is just condemnation."* (*Faith of the Early Fathers*, by W. A. Jurgens)

St. Thomas Aquinas said, *"The Saints do not pray for deceased unbelievers and wicked men, knowing them to already be condemned to eternal and irrevocable damnation."* (*Summa Theologica*)

St. Francis Xavier said, *"Before their baptism, certain Japanese were greatly troubled by a hateful scruple: that God did not appear merciful, because he had never made himself known to the Japanese people before, especially that those who had not worshipped God were doomed to everlasting Hell. They grieve over the fate of their departed children, parents, relatives; so they ask if there is anyway to free them by prayer from their eternal misery. And I am obliged to answer: there is absolutely none."* (Letter from Japan, to the Society of Jesus in Europe, 1552)

St. Louis Marie De Montfort: *"My heart is penetrated with grief when I think of the almost infinite number of souls who are damned for lack of knowing the true God and the Christian religion. The greatest misfortune, O my God, is not to know Thee, and the greatest punishment not to love Thee."* (Love of Eternal Wisdom)

However, God could infuse good-willed men who do love God with the Faith at sometime immediately before or at death, whoever they may be that are in error. At this point, the individual would not be holding on to false religious beliefs. If God wants to save someone who pleases Him, then He can do it. Non-Catholics cannot be saved as non-Catholics, but as ex-non-Catholics.

Those who live as Protestants or Eastern Orthodox but never actually rejected Catholicism are not actual Protestants or Eastern Orthodox. If they have a valid Baptism, then they are material heretics, which are Catholics in error.

Objection 15: *"All those truths must be believed fide Divina et Catholica, which are contained in the written word of God, either by a solemn definition or through her ordinary and universal teaching. To pronounce a solemn definition is the part of an ecumenical council or of the Roman Pontiff speaking ex cathedra. No religious teaching is to be understood as dogmatically declared unless such declaration or definition has clearly been made."* Pope Martin V at the Council of Constance in his Apostolic Constitiution, *Inter Cuntas*, Feb.22, 1418, ARTICLE 11

Pope Pius IX, First Vatican Council, Sess. 3, Chap. 2 *on Revelation*, 1870, *ex cathedra*: *"Hence, also, that understanding of its sacred dogmas must be perpetually retained, which Holy Mother Church has once declared; and there must never be a recession from that meaning under the specious name of a deeper understanding."*

Therefore, Baptism of Desire and Blood adds to the dogma and even changes it, thus making it recede.

Vatican 1 laid out 5 criteria of papal infallibility: 1. Speaking as pope and not as a mere theologian. 2. Must be doctrinal. 3. Must be on faith and morals. 4. Must be speaking universally to the whole church. 5. Must let us know that this is a definition that must be believed which could never be revoked.

Let's hypothetically say some modernists didn't like the dogma of the Immaculate Conception. So they try to add another criteria to papal infallibility. As a hypothetical proposition, of course, they would say that the pope must write the doctrine down in these three languages: Greek, Latin, and Hebrew.

Now, one would have to look in history to see what doctrines were defined by popes that fit all 6 of the criteria. Only those would be infallible while the rest were not and therefore not binding in the same

> way. This could not happen because this would not be a development of doctrine, but an evolution of doctrine. Today, we have modernists who despise the doctrine of outside the church there is no salvation, so now we see exceptions trying to creep in to mean that those outside the church are really inside the Church as long as they have implicit faith. This is not true development but an evolution of doctrine.

Baptism of Desire and Blood does not add to or change the dogma, but explains how the dogma is to be understood under extraordinary conditions.

To say that those who have implicit faith are really inside the Church is incorrect. Implicit faith alone does not get you inside the Church. It takes much more and even then God would have to make it happen.

The use of this objection would solemnly condemn St. Alphonsus Liquori and Pope St. Pius X as formal heretics for sure.

> **Objection 16:** It is a theological opinion at best, I don't have to believe it to be Catholic.

The First Vatican Council taught:

*[**The object of faith**]. Further, **by divine and Catholic faith, all those things must be believed** which are contained in the written word of God and in tradition, and those which are proposed by the Church, either in a solemn pronouncement or in **her ordinary and universal teaching power, to be believed as divinely revealed.*** (Dogmatic Constitution concerning the Catholic Faith, Ch. 3, FIRST VATICAN COUNCIL, Pope Pius IX) (Denz. 1792)

A dogma comes from a solemn pronouncement, but all ordinary and universal teachings must also be held as being divinely revealed.

BOD (the possibility of being saved apart from the Sacrament of Baptism) falls under the ordinary and universal magisterial teaching.

The high majority of Church Fathers, including popes, teach it and it is actually asserted in Canon Law, because it is taught at the Council of Trent and implied at the Council of Florence.

A Catholic who knowingly does not believe in Vatican I, meaning that he only believes in the dogmatic pronouncements but not the ordinary and universal teachings, is a heretic.

The hundreds of Encyclicals written by popes for the whole Church that do not define any dogma would be meaningless.

A Catholic could not ignore them or reject them just because they are not dogmatic. If so, then why would the pope go to the trouble of teaching anything non-dogmatic at all, if the faithful are not bound to it? What's the purpose?

BOD IS THE TEACHING THAT IT IS POSSIBLE TO BE SAVED APART FROM THE SACRAMENT.

As a side note: Even by wearing the Brown Scapular, Our Lady's promise to save all who die wearing it stays intact because it allows this possibility that Our Lady obtains those things I mentioned as the means to be saved as the teaching of BOD would require: Final penitence, perfect contrition, and the desire of the Sacrament.

There cannot be a contradiction, and the Church can't give us one.

Since BOD falls under the universal and ordinary teaching, it cannot be doubted. It must be held as Vatican I says all of these types of teachings must be held as being divinely revealed. BOD has not been defined dogmatically or in its entirety, but so far the Church has taught one aspect of it. It is possible to be saved apart from water under certain circumstances. Exactly how it all works precisely can be speculated, doubted, questioned, etc. BOD must be accepted this much.

Objection 17: Secondly, God often will punish a soul or damn a soul as an example for others. Many in the Old Testament were killed directly by God immediately after just one sin. The priests who used the unconsecrated matches at the altar, and the one who tried to stop the Ark of the Covenant from tilting over, and the act of Schism by Core and his followers. And then we read this from Scripture about Sodom and Gomorrah.

"And reducing the cities of the Sodomites and of the Gomorrahites into ashes, condemned them to be overthrown, making them an example to those that should after act wickedly..." (II Peter 2:2)

So it would not seem out of the realm of possibility that God would let a soul perish on the way to being baptized if only to perhaps warn others not to procrastinate with their baptism.

This objection doesn't apply to BOD especially under the rubric of Trent's Catechism. Catechumens were not procrastinating, but the Church was for good reasons. For those other than catechumens, it would depend upon God and whom He wants to save and who pleases Him. Perhaps, some procrastinators will be lost, but some may not be.

Objection 18: Against Baptism of Blood was Pope Pelagius II (A.D. 578 - 590) Epistle 585: *"Consider the fact that whoever has not been in the peace and unity of the Church cannot have the Lord. ...Although given over to flames and fires, they burn, or, thrown to wild beasts, they lay down their lives, there will not be (for them) that crown of faith but the punishment of faithlessness. ...Such a one can be slain, he cannot be crowned. ...[If] slain outside the Church, he cannot attain the rewards of the Church."*

And the Bull of Eugene IV. *"No one, let his almsgiving be as great as it may, no one, even if he pour out his blood for the Name of Christ, can be saved, unless he remain within the bosom and the unity of the Catholic Church."* (Pope Eugene IV, the Bull *Cantate Domino*, 1441.)

Pope Pelagius is saying that if one is slain outside the Church because he has not been in the peace and unity of the Church, he will not go to Heaven. This is true. It doesn't apply at all to the doctrine of Baptism of Blood.

Baptism of Blood is for those who never were in the Church but desires to be in peace and unity with the Church.

As for the Bull *Cantate Domino*, the shedding of blood for Jesus will do nothing for you if you leave the Church. This is the clear meaning of the Bull. It presumes one was in the Church to begin with and left. Pope Pelagius and Pope Eugene are saying the same thing.

It is not referring to the doctrine of BOD or Baptism by Blood, for both teach that one wants to be united to the Church. The Bull is referring to those who do not want to be within the Church.

Objection 19: Concerning baptism, Pope Clement XI said, *"A missionary should not baptize one who does not believe explicitly in the Lord Jesus Christ, but is bound to instruct him about all those matters which are necessary, by a necessity of means, in accordance with the capacity of the one to be baptized."* [Response of the Sacred Office, May 10 1703] D-1349b
Why would explicit faith be needed to baptize a pagan but implicit faith of a pagan is good enough for salvation anyway? Why worry about whether the pagan has implicit faith or explicit faith if he has explicit desire? This letter simply confirms that explicit faith is needed to be saved. Implicit faith won't do it.

A pagan doesn't have explicit faith, but an ex-pagan catechuman does.

The Sacrament of Baptism is never to be administered to an adult who does not have explicit faith. The whole point is that explicit faith for an adult must be present for Baptism to justify the sinner. Baptism alone doesn't save a sinner. The penalty would be far worse if a sinner entered Hell with the Mark of Baptism than without it. Faith is the necessity of means along with Baptism.

The missionary is responsible before God to do the right thing and he is responsible for the soul.

Explicit desire to be baptized is not good enough. As just been noted, explicit faith is the necessity of means. Anybody may want to be baptized, but may want it for the wrong reasons. The missionary can never know, but he could make a better assessment by whether the one with explicit desire also has explicit faith.

Now implicit faith is not good enough alone and a pagan cannot be saved as a pagan no matter what. BOD is the teaching that God can save apart from the Sacrament for those who are of goodwill provided they are perfectly contrite, and desire to be with God. In cases of those without explicit faith, which is the necessity of means, the implicit faith must be one where explicit faith is not possible under ordinary conditions, whereby the necessity of means would then not be one of explicit faith. Only God knows them, and He must infuse that explicit Faith.

The circumstances depend on what is necessary and what is not. These are why the ordinary means and extraordinary means require the different modes of necessity.

> **Objection 20:** I Tim. 2:4 says, *"God desires all men to be saved."* If God's desire doesn't or can't actually save us, why would our desire by itself can? If it is our desire united to God's desire that does the trick, then the externals of our faith would be superfluous especially the Sacraments. Most everyone sincerely desires to be saved. Even the atheist would say, *"If God does exist, I most certainly would want to be with him and not in hell."* As long as none of them are in mortal sin, then all of them would go to heaven. The Gospel would just be a help and not actually necessary.

An atheist doesn't say this because he firmly claims to believe in no God. An agnostic however, might say this, but he has no excuse to be an agnostic as St. Paul says in Romans 1:18-20. He is in the same boat as the claimed atheist. Both will be lost in the end because it is a mortal sin to be an atheist or agnostic.

God may desire all men to be saved but not all men desire to be saved. God allows man to choose, He doesn't force it upon him. The Council of Trent addresses this by refuting Calvinism.

Calvinism teaches the prelapsarian Adam never had infused grace but was on his own, putting him in a covenant of works. When

Adam fell, he was completely without grace; dead as it were (or totally depraved). Catholicism teaches the prelapsarian Adam had infused grace to help him make the right decision and after the fall had residual grace; injured as it were (or depraved but not totally). This residual grace or prevenient grace helps man cooperate with God. This is why Calvinists claim Catholics are semi-Pelagian. Calvinists fail to recognize that Catholics believe the fallen Adam had residual infused grace. It is synergism but not all synergism. God is always working in man, but leaving the man free to act. This is a mystery.

Calvinists teach that God alone does it all. If man is totally depraved he must be completely made alive. He cannot cooperate since a dead man cannot do anything. When made alive, he cannot dissent because he does not and will not want to dissent. Though Calvinists will not admit to it, man is programmed in their theology. After God acts on the man, he will choose God regardless. Calvinists will say he freely chose but in actuality, he freely chose precisely because God made it so by His effectual grace. Calvinist may claim man always has free will, but really it is a thing only in name, indeed a name without a reality, a fiction introduced into the Church by Satan as the Council of Trent identified in Canon 5 of the 6th session.

Our desire united to God's desire does not make the externals of our faith superfluous because the Sacraments are the means to live in grace under ordinary conditions. It is no trick.

Objection 21: Outside the Church there is no salvation only would only apply to Catholics who knowingly leave the Church since they are the only ones who are not ignorant. Everyone else would have salvation by avoiding mortal sin and wanting to be saved.

Catholics can be saved only if they practice the faith without doubt, fast, give, and do all the church commands, but the invincibly ignorant just has to be sincere and follow his conscience. This is absurd.

The issue is never about EENS. This is the common straw-man argument.

As for mortal sin, avoiding it for very long would be nearly impossible without the Church. It would take an extraordinary amount of actual grace. Merely wanting to be saved does not at all apply to BOD.

It is true that Catholics must work hard for their salvation.

Christ said in Luke 12: 48, *"But he who did not know, and did what deserved a beating, shall receive a light beating. Every one to whom much is given, of him will much be required; and of him to whom men commit much they will demand the more."*

This only means that God may have prepared a higher place for those who have been given the Faith throughout their lives.

The invincibly ignorant must be very sincere in trying to please God, and live honest lives, always willing to obey God. Their only help is the law written on their hearts and sound reasoning. If they can do that (and they can only by the grace of God), then God can provide the supernatural means of saving them in the end by infusing in them the Faith whereby, they would no longer be ignorant.

The implication of this objection is that it is much easier for the invincibly ignorant when in fact the Catholic may have to work harder, but the invincibly ignorant will have a much harder time achieving the same goal.

There would be no point in evangelizing, if conversion to Christ made it harder for one to be saved.

Catholics living and working out their salvation have a good hope of being saved. Non-Catholics do not have any hope of being saved, unless there is a miracle from God who must infuse in them the Catholic Faith. This is what Baptism of Desire is, a supernatural miracle.

Objection 22: The letter attributed to Pope Innocent II as *Apostolicam Sedem* is probably a forgery. It has no real authority since we can't be sure who actually wrote it. Some attribute it to Pope Innocent III. Its basis is on the sole testimony of Ambrose and

> Augustine. It is written to an un-named bishop and not to the whole church. This letter proves nothing.

St. Alphonsus Liquori completely disagrees since he considered it a de fide teaching based on this letter, as it was part of the canon in his day. Therefore, the Church recognized it.

Some people say there are some Holy Scriptures that are forgeries, because they are not sure who wrote them while based solely on the testimony of certain saints. However, the Church recognized them as well as *Apostolicam* of Pope Innocent II.

However, the point is that we have a pope who believes and teaches BOD.

> **Objection 23:** Pope Innocent III's letter to a Bishop Berthold of Metz on August 28, 1206, is simply erroneous. It is not binding since it is not part of the universal and ordinary teaching of the Magisterium.

This is a valid point that it is not binding, but not erroneous. However, this is another example of a pope who believes and teaches BOD.

> **Objection 24:** In Pope Pius IX, *Singulari Quidem*, On the Church in Austria Encyclical, March 17, 1856, which states, *"[17] Outside of the Church, nobody can hope for life or salvation unless he is excused through ignorance beyond his control."*
>
> He never says that those excused will we be saved, but that they can hope. But it doesn't matter since this is not an encyclical but an address. It is not binding.

The point is missed. How can those excused by invincible ignorance hope, if there is no hope for them? This makes no sense. It may not be binding, but it proves that Pope Pius IX clearly believed in the teachings of BOD.

Invincible ignorance does not save, but those in ignorance will be excused for not having the Catholic Faith throughout their life. If they live honest lives always being open to God's Grace and willing to please Him. God will avail them supernatural grace and infuse them the Faith to be saved.

> **Objection 25:** In Pope Pius IX, *Quanto Conficiamur Moerore*, On Promotion of False Doctrines Encyclical, August 10, 1863, He specifically condemns the idea that a man *"living in error and separated from the true Faith"* can be saved. The very concept of salvation for the *"invincibly ignorant"* is condemned here.
>
> Pope Pius IX does not say anywhere that the invincibly ignorant can be saved where they are. Rather, he is reiterating that the ignorant, if they cooperate with God's grace, keep the natural law and respond to God's call, they can by God attain eternal life, since God will certainly bring all of his elect to the knowledge of the truth and into the Church by baptism.
>
> This is the clear meaning of his statement.

Baptism of Desire does not say invincibly ignorant can be saved where they are.

This objection says those invincibly ignorant will be baptized if they cooperate with God's grace, keep the natural law, and respond to God's call, but this in not what the pope says. If Pius IX meant Baptism he most certainly would have stated so, but he didn't. He was clearly referring to those who will never know the Faith under ordinary conditions. According to Pius IX, *"They... can attain eternal life"*, but not by Baptism, but *"by the efficacious virtue of divine light and grace."*

This is BOD made clear.

The staunchest of all apologists on the Catholic Dogma EENS was Fr. Michael Müller C.SS.R. (1825 – 1899). He always submitted his works to two Redemptorist theologians (as his rule required) and to his religious superiors before publication.

One of his many great Catholic books titled *"The Catholic Dogma"* defended the Church's teaching of BOD. He wrote that an invincibly ignorant person cannot be saved by his ignorance, but can be saved outside the Sacrament of Baptism. He also defended the true meaning of Pope Pius IX's teaching on this topic.

Fr. Michael Müller, C.SS.R., The Catholic Dogma, pp. 217-218, 1888:

"Inculpable or invincible ignorance has never been and will never be a means of salvation. To be saved, it is necessary to be justified, or to be in the state of grace. In order to obtain sanctifying grace, it is necessary to have the proper dispositions for justification; that is, true divine faith in at least the necessary truths of salvation, confident hope in the divine Savior, sincere sorrow for sin, together with the firm purpose of doing all that God has commanded, etc. Now, these supernatural acts of faith, hope, charity, contrition, etc., which prepare the soul for receiving sanctifying grace, can never be supplied by invincible ignorance; and if invincible ignorance cannot supply the preparation for receiving sanctifying grace, much less can it bestow sanctifying grace itself. 'Invincible ignorance,' says St. Thomas, 'is a punishment for sin.' (De, Infid. Q. x., art. 1). "It is, then, a curse, but not a blessing or a means of salvation… Hence Pius IX said 'that, were a man to be invincibly ignorant of the true religion, such invincible ignorance would not be sinful before God; that, if such a person should observe the precepts of the Natural Law and do the will of God to the best of his knowledge, God, in his infinite mercy, may enlighten him so as to obtain eternal life; for, the Lord who knows the heart and the thoughts of man will, in his infinite goodness, not suffer anyone to be lost forever without his own fault.' Almighty God, who is just condemns no one without his fault, puts, therefore, such souls as are in invincible ignorance of the truths of salvation, in the way of salvation, either by natural or supernatural means."

Fr. Michael Müller also wrote a catechism titled *"Familiar Explanation of Christian Doctrine."* He writes:

Q. What are we to think of the salvation of those who are out of the pale of the Church without any fault of theirs, and who never had any opportunity of knowing better?

A. Their inculpable ignorance will not save them; but if they fear God and live up to their conscience, God, in His infinite mercy, will furnish them with the necessary means of salvation, even so as to send, if needed, an angel to instruct them in the Catholic faith, rather than let them perish through inculpable ignorance.

Q. Is it then right for us to say that one who was not received into the Church before his death, is damned?

A. No.

Q. Why not?

A. Because we cannot know for certain what takes place between God and the soul at the awful moment of death.

Q. What do you mean by this?

A. I mean that God, in His infinite mercy, may enlighten, at the hour of death, one who is not yet a Catholic, so that he may see the truth of the Catholic faith, be truly sorry for his sins, and sincerely desire to die a good Catholic.

Q. What do we say of those who receive such an extraordinary grace, and die in this manner?

A. We say of them that they die united, at least, to the soul of the Catholic Church, and are saved.

Q. What, then, awaits all those who are out of the Catholic Church, and die without having received such an extraordinary grace at the hour of death?

A. Eternal damnation.

Pope Pius IX and Fr. Müller have just expounded the doctrine of Baptism of Desire perfectly.

Objection 26: Catechism of St. Pius X written by Pope St. Pius X is clearly in error and should be rejected on this point SEE OBJECTION 27

The problem with this objection is it necessarily makes Pope St. Pius X a formal heretic and ipso facto not a pope. He cannot be excused with ignorance of the teachings of the Church.

However, this explanation follows all the other catechisms and does not reject the dogma EENS. It follows the teaching of Pope Pius IX of *Quanto Conficiamur Moerore*.

This catechism is so damning to those who oppose BOD that they will go so far as to claim that Pope St. Pius X never wrote it.

> **Objection 27:** Pope Leo XIII, *Satis Cognitum* (# 3), June 29, 1896: *"For this reason the Church is so often called in Holy Writ a body, and even the body of Christ... From this it follows that those who arbitrarily conjure up and picture to themselves a hidden and invisible Church are in grievous and pernicious error... It is assuredly impossible that the Church of Jesus Christ can be the one or the other, as that man should be a body alone or a soul alone. The connection and union of both elements is as absolutely necessary to the true Church as the intimate union of the soul and body is to human nature. The Church is not something dead: it is the body of Christ endowed with supernatural life."*
>
> This means you cannot be united to the Soul of the Church if you are not a member of the Body of the Church.

Pope Leo was arguing against those who reject the Church as a visible Body or human institution and those who reject the Church as a divine institution.

In fact, the Church is the mystical Body of Christ, which is both human and divine.

As Pope Leo states, it has *"visible and invisible elements."*

The Church is not separated in its elements but one could be united to one of the elements and not the other.

71

A Catholic in mortal sin is united to the body of the Church but not the soul. He is physically alive, but spiritually dead. Both the body and the soul of the Church are alive and the soul is what gives life to its members. Being spiritually dead would be a separation from the soul of the Church.

Therefore, one can indeed be separated from the body of the Church, but united to the soul of the Church.

> **Objection 28:** The story about St. Alban and his guard has and incorrect conclusion. The guard was baptized because of another account from Bede and Butler's Lives of the Saints reveals a miraculous spring.
>
> St. Bede: *As he reached the summit, holy Alban asked God to give him (Alban) water, and at once a perennial spring bubbled up at his feet..."*
>
> Butler: *"The sudden conversion of the headsmen occasioned a delay in the execution. In the meantime the holy confessor (Alban), with the crowd, went up the hill...There Alban falling on his knees, at his prayer a fountain sprung up, with water whereof he refreshed his thirst... Together with St. Alban, the soldier, who had refused to imbrue (stain) his hands in his blood, and had declared himself a Christian, was also beheaded, being baptized in his own blood."*
>
> The water was for baptism not to refresh thirst. This is the obvious reason for the miraculous spring.

The problem is that Bede and Butler would have easily have noticed this point if it were true. The fact is they tell the story knowing full well that the story was to describe the fact that Baptism of Blood is what happened.

Those bent on rejecting Baptism of Blood have to make out Bede and Butler as real dummies, and to do whatever it takes to prove it wrong, even if it means taking the plain meaning out of a story by the very ones who tell it for that very purpose.

> **Objection 29:** To say un-Baptized infants can be saved by Baptism of Blood goes directly against Pope Eugene IV, Council of Florence, Session 11, Feb. 4, 1442:
>
> *"Regarding children, indeed, because of danger of death, which can often take place, when no help can be brought to them by another remedy than through the sacrament of baptism, through which they are snatched from the domination of the Devil [original sin] and adopted among the sons of God." And the Catechism of Trent, which says, "no other means of salvation than baptism."*

This does not go against the Council of Florence since being martyred is not a remedy.

It does not go against the Roman Catechism, since the Catechism wasn't referring to this particular extraordinary condition. There is no other means of salvation than Baptism under normal circumstances, since infants cannot desire to be saved. The Catechism wasn't referring to this particular situation of martyrdom.

St. Alphonsus, *Moral Theology*, Bk. 6, nn. 95-97: *"Baptism of blood is the shedding of one's blood, i.e. death, suffered for the faith or for some other Christian virtue. Now this Baptism is comparable to true baptism because, like true Baptism, it remits both guilt and punishment as it were ex opere operato...Hence martyrdom avails also for infants seeing that the Church venerates the Holy Innocents as true martyrs. That is why Suarez rightly teaches that the opposing view is at least temerarious."*

The Holy Innocents were saved under the Old Testament, and to say that such could not be saved under the New Testament, which is under God's grace is absurd and probably blasphemous.

> **Objection 30:** God allowed the war to stop short Vatican I to keep it from falling into error with defining Baptism of Desire and Blood.

Pius IX gives official magisterial approval of this widely held opinion in his encyclical when he excludes from salvation only those who are contumaciously and pertinacious divided from the churches unity.

The most prominent theologian of the day, Giovanni Perrone strongly held to the teaching of BOD/BOD. His theology is clearly given Papal approval By Pius IX. Perrone was unequivocal in his belief of BOD/BOB as were then most Catholic Theologians worldwide.

Another famous theologian and priest, Father Johann Franzelin S. J. was a priest who taught at the Roman college until 1876.

Franzelin, from his piece, *'Theses de Ecclesia Christi*, Thesis 24, states:

"Since justification occurs only through supernatural faith and, as St. Paul teaches, 'faith comes through what is heard' [Romans 10:17], the saving message must be proclaimed — the task of the Church. Furthermore, faith orients a person to the Church and even if that person will not be joined to the Church on earth, he is oriented toward the eschatological Church, to which the earthly Church is intimately and indissolubly bound. Beyond that, those not in communion with the Catholic Church, by virtue of their desire for salvation, have at least an implicit desire for such membership. In short, anyone who is destined for salvation, achieves that goal through the Church and by a relationship with her... Such people (invincibly ignorant) are not saved except through the church, to which the word of faith belongs, and in view of which saving graces are given; and they are not saved except in the church, insofar as they are united not only to her spirit but also to her visible elements by their will, which is accepted by God in lieu of the fact...........Thus in the eyes of God and the church triumphant, there is no justification without union with the church on earth."

This analysis is the first draft of the Constitution on the Church proposed at Vatican I; due to the outbreak of the Franco-Prussian War, however, this document was tabled as the Council adjourned.

Pope Pius IX being the pope that presided over that council allowed the draft that defended the teaching of BOD and BOB to be considered.

Instead of correcting him, Pope Pius IX elevates Father Franzelin, who was teaching this doctrine publicly under his nose at the Roman College, to the ranks of cardinal in 1876.

This would necessarily make Pope Pius IX a terrible heretic and antipope or an absolute fool.

> **Objection 31:** The Church may have not condemned those false teachings from the catechisms and the saints, but that doesn't mean the doctrine is true.
>
> No pope ever ordered the false belief that Mary was conceived in sin to be removed from St. Thomas Aquinas, *Summa Theologica*, Pt. III, Q, A. 3, Reply to Objection 1.
>
> The false belief of BOD/BOB was allowed to manifest those who would believe the heresy.
>
> *"For there must be also heresies; that they also, who are approved, may be manifest among you."* I Cor. 11:19

The problem with this objection is that the supposed heresy of BOD/BOB is coming from the authority of the Church itself and not from the lay members.

The Breviary acknowledges and promotes the belief of saints who were baptized by blood. Thousands of the clergy have been reading and praying with it for many years. Not one questioned it. It doesn't even matter if these saints were not actually baptized by blood as those who argue so, because it is a presumed fact that they did and the Church has been promoting it the whole time. The recognizing of saints by the Church is infallible.

St. Alphonsus Liquori could not be recognized as a saint since he would have been a heretic for believing that the doctrine was de fide despite the words of Our Lord and papal teaching.

The Catholic Encyclopedia, Vol. 2, "Beatification," 1907, p. 366: *"In Quodlib. IX, a. 16, St. Thomas says: 'Since the honor we pay the saints is in a certain sense a profession of faith, i.e., a belief in the glory of the Saints, we must piously believe that in this matter also the Church is not liable to error."*

St. Alphonsus Liguori, The Great Means of Salvation and Perfection, 1759, p. 23, states: *"To suppose that the Church can err in canonizing, is a sin, or is heresy, according to St. Bonaventure, Bellarmine, and others; or at least next door to heresy, according to Suarez, Azorius, Gotti, etc.; because the Sovereign Pontiff, according to St. Thomas, is guided by the infallible influence of the Holy Ghost in an especial way when canonizing saints."*

Yet, it is because the Church believes these saints died from the Baptism of Blood that makes them saints.

St. Francis De Sales: (+1602): *"...to say the Church errs is to say no less that God errs, or else that He is willing and desirous for us to err; which would be a great blasphemy."* (*The Catholic Controversy*, p. 70.)

In fact, the Church has done nothing but encourage the belief in the doctrine of BOD/BOB everywhere you look.

It is found in the Breviary, Catechisms, the 1917 Code of Canon Law, the encyclicals, and many writings of the Saints and Doctors of the Church. It's everywhere!

This objection fails to see the obvious!

As for St. Thomas Aquinas, the dogma of the Immaculate Conception was not yet defined, and this particular dogma is very implicit in Scripture and Tradition. The Church needs not to remove it from his writing because we all know the truth.

Therefore, the Scripture verse in I Cor. 11:19 is a double-edge sword. It could be used precisely for those who reject the truth of Baptism of Desire and Blood to manifest them as the real heretics.

> **Objection 32:** The Council of Trent says Justification can be attained by a person with the Catholic Faith together with at least a desire for the Sacraments. He cannot attain Salvation unless he receives the Sacraments.
>
> As the foregoing discussion from the Council of Trent points out, justification and salvation are two different things. Justification is the road to salvation, and not salvation itself. After all, we are Catholics who believe in a dogmatic faith, good works, and sanctifying grace, not Protestants who believe in confidence alone!

It is true that Justification and Salvation are two distinct things, but in the end you can't have one without the other. Justification is the road to salvation but it also is the cause of salvation.

The Council of Trent refutes in Session VI, Chapter 7. *"The causes of this justification are; the final cause indeed is the glory of God and of Christ and life eternal."*

The point of Baptism is to become justified so that one can be saved. Justification causes salvation for the one justified.

To follow through with this form of logic, the one dies justified but without Baptism will not go to Heaven and he cannot go to Hell.

> **Objection 33:** Salvation can come only through the Sacrament of Baptism is a very hard saying, and it not us who are bent on rejecting BOD/BOB, but it is you who are bent on disproving the plain words of Our Lord. Our position requires more faith for having to just accept that salvation is not possible any other way but through the Sacrament of Baptism.

Atheism also requires more faith because it goes against sound logic. Calvinism requires more faith because it relies on a trust with no foundation. Islam requires much more faith since it is based totally on the teaching of Mohammed who claims to have been given the faith by an angel. If Mohammed were telling the truth about the angel, then the faith of Muslims also must rest in trusting that the angel came from God and not from hell. Thus they must totally put their trust in those two sources alone. What a weak foundation for the religion that ultimately will determine the fate of one's eternal life!

All these require more faith, but uses false reasoning.

BOB/BOB uses sound reasoning, where as to object to it requires false reasoning having with it false conclusions.

The purpose of this writing is in showing that fact.

APPENDIX 1 - OUTSIDE THE CHURCH THERE IS NO SALVATION.

Pope St. Hormisdas, (514-523) *Book on the Profession of Faith*, D. 171: "The first condition of salvation is to keep the norm of the true faith and in no way to deviate from the established doctrine of the Fathers."

Pope St. Gregory the Great, quoted in *Summo Iugiter Studio*, 590-604: "The holy universal Church teaches that it is not possible to worship God truly except in her and asserts that all who are outside of her will not be saved."

Pope Adrain II, (867-872) ACTIO I, D. 171, n.1, quoting the Rule of Pope St. Hormisdas, IV Constantinople: "The first requirement of salvation is to keep to the standard of the true faith."

Pope Innocent III, *Eius exemplo*, Dec. 18, 1208: "By the heart we believe and by the mouth we confess the one Church, not of heretics, but the Holy Roman, Catholic, and Apostolic Church outside of which we believe that no one is saved."

Pope Innocent III, Fourth Lateran Council, *Constitution* 1, 1215: "There is indeed one universal Church of the faithful, outside of which nobody at all is saved, in which Jesus Christ is both priest and sacrifice."

Pope Boniface VIII, *Unam Sanctam*, Nov. 18, 1302: "With Faith urging us we are forced to believe and to hold the one, holy, Catholic Church and that, apostolic, and we firmly believe and simply confess this Church outside of which there is no salvation nor remission of sin...Furthermore, we declare, say, define, and proclaim to every human creature that they by absolute necessity for salvation are entirely subject to the Roman Pontiff."

Pope Clement V, Council of Vienne, Decree # 30, 1311-1312: "Since however there is for both regulars and seculars, for superiors and subjects, for exempt and non-exempt, one universal Church, outside of which there is no salvation, for all of whom there is one Lord, one faith, and one baptism..."

Pope Clement VI, *Super quibusdam*, Sept. 20, 1351: "In the second place, we ask whether you and the Armenians obedient to you believe that no man of the wayfarers outside the faith of this Church, and outside the obedience to the Pope of Rome, can finally be saved."

Pope Eugene IV, Council of Florence, Sess. 8, Nov. 22, 1439: "Whoever wishes to be saved, needs above all to hold the Catholic faith; unless each one preserves this whole and inviolate, he will without a doubt perish in eternity."

Pope Eugene IV, Council of Florence, *"Cantate Domino,"* 1441: "The Holy Roman Church firmly believes, professes and preaches that all those who are outside the Catholic Church, not only pagans but also Jews or heretics and schismatics, cannot share in eternal life and will go into the everlasting fire which was prepared for the devil and his angels, unless they are joined to the Church before the end of their lives; that the unity of this ecclesiastical body is of such importance that only for those who abide in it do the Church's sacraments contribute to salvation and do fasts, almsgiving and other works of piety and practices of the Christian militia produce eternal rewards; and that nobody can be saved, no matter how much he has given away in alms and even if he has shed blood in the name of Christ, unless he has persevered in the bosom and unity of the Catholic Church."

Pope Leo X, Fifth Lateran Council, Session 11, Dec. 19, 1516: "For, regulars and seculars, prelates and subjects, exempt and non-exempt, belong to the one universal Church, outside of which no one at all is saved, and they all have one Lord and one faith."

Pope Pius IV, Council of Trent, *"Iniunctum nobis,"* Nov. 13, 1565: "This true Catholic faith, outside of which no one can be saved... I now profess and truly hold..."

Pope St. Pius V, Bull excommunicating the heretic Queen Elizabeth of England, Feb. 25, 1570: "The sovereign jurisdiction of the one holy

Catholic and Apostolic Church, outside of which there is no salvation, has been given by Him [Jesus Christ], unto Whom all power in Heaven and on Earth is given, the King who reigns on high, but to one person on the face of the Earth, to Peter, prince of the Apostles... If any shall contravene this Our decree, we bind them with the same bond of anathema."

Pope Benedict XIV, *Nuper ad nos*, March 16, 1743, Profession of Faith: "This faith of the Catholic Church, without which no one can be saved, and which of my own accord I now profess and truly hold…"

Pope Leo XII, *Ubi Primum* (# 14), May 5, 1824: "It is impossible for the most true God, who is Truth itself, the best, the wisest Provider, and the Rewarder of good men, to approve all sects who profess false teachings which are often inconsistent with one another and contradictory, and to confer eternal rewards on their members... by divine faith we hold one Lord, one faith, one baptism... This is why we profess that there is no salvation outside the Church."

Pope Leo XII, *Quod hoc ineunte* (# 8), May 24, 1824: "We address all of you who are still removed from the true Church and the road to salvation. In this universal rejoicing, one thing is lacking: that having been called by the inspiration of the Heavenly Spirit and having broken every decisive snare, you might sincerely agree with the mother Church, outside of whose teachings there is no salvation."

Pope Gregory XVI, *Summo Iugiter Studio* (# 2), May 27, 1832: "Finally some of these misguided people attempt to persuade themselves and others that men are not saved only in the Catholic religion, but that even heretics may attain eternal life."

Pope Gregory XVI, *Mirari Vos* (# 13), Aug. 15, 1832: "With the admonition of the apostle, that 'there is one God, one faith, one baptism' (Eph. 4:5), may those fear who contrive the notion that the safe harbor of salvation is open to persons of any religion whatever. They should consider the testimony of Christ Himself that 'those who are not with Christ are against Him,' (Lk. 11:23) and that they disperse unhappily who do not gather with Him. Therefore, 'without a doubt, they will perish forever, unless they hold the Catholic faith whole and inviolate (Athanasian Creed)."

Pope Gregory XVI, (A.D. 1831 - 1846) Encyclical, *Summo Jugiter*: "It is not possible to worship God truly except in Her; all who are outside Her will not be saved."

Pope Pius IX, *Ubi primum* (# 10), June 17, 1847: "For 'there is one universal Church outside of which no one at all is saved; it contains regular and secular prelates along with those under their jurisdiction, who all profess one Lord, one faith and one baptism."

Pope Pius IX, *Nostis et Nobiscum* (# 10), Dec. 8, 1849: "In particular, ensure that the faithful are deeply and thoroughly convinced of the truth of the doctrine that the Catholic faith is necessary for attaining salvation. (This doctrine, received from Christ and emphasized by the Fathers and Councils, is also contained in the formulae of the profession of faith used by Latin, Greek and Oriental Catholics)."

Pope Pius IX, *Syllabus of Modern Errors*, Dec. 8, 1864 Proposition 16: "Man may, in the observance of any religion whatever, find the way of eternal salvation, and arrive at eternal salvation." – Condemned

Pope Pius IX, Vatican Council I, Session 2, *Profession of Faith*, 1870, *ex cathedra*: "This true Catholic faith, outside of which none can be saved, which I now freely profess and truly hold..."

Pope Leo XIII, *Tametsi futura prospicientibus* (# 7), Nov. 1, 1900: "Christ is man's 'Way'; the Church also is his 'Way'... Hence all who would find salvation apart from the Church, are led astray and strive in vain."

Pope St. Pius X, *Iucunda sane* (# 9), March 12, 1904: "Yet at the same time We cannot but remind all, great and small, as Pope St. Gregory did, of the absolute necessity of having recourse to this Church in order to have eternal salvation..."

Pope St. Pius X, *Editae saepe* (# 29), May 26, 1910: "The Church alone possesses together with her magisterium the power of governing and sanctifying human society. Through her ministers and servants (each in his own station and office), she confers on mankind suitable and necessary means of salvation."

Pope Pius XI, *Mortalium Animos* (# 11), Jan. 6, 1928: "The Catholic Church is alone in keeping the true worship. This is the fount of truth, this is the house of faith, this is the temple of God: if any man enter not here, or if any man go forth from it, he is a stranger to the hope of life and salvation."

Pope Pius XII, *Mystici Corporis Christi* (# 41), June 29, 1943: "They, therefore, walk in the path of dangerous error who believe that they can accept Christ as the Head of the Church, while not adhering loyally to His Vicar on earth. They have taken away the visible head, broken the visible bonds of unity and left the Mystical Body of the Redeemer so obscured and so maimed, that those who are seeking the haven of eternal salvation can neither see it nor find it."

APPENDIX 2 - NECESSITY OF BAPTISM AND/OR FAITH

Pope Clement V, Council of Vienne, 1311-1312, *ex cathedra*: "Besides, one baptism which regenerates all who are baptized in Christ must be faithfully confessed by all just as 'one God and one faith' [Eph. 4:5], which celebrated in water in the name of the Father and of the Son and of the Holy Spirit we believe to be commonly the perfect remedy for salvation for adults as for children."

Pope Eugene IV, The Council of Florence, *"Exultate Deo,"* Nov. 22, 1439, *ex cathedra*: "Holy baptism, which is the gateway to the spiritual life, holds the first place among all the sacraments; through it we are made members of Christ and of the body of the Church. And since death entered the universe through the first man, 'unless we are born again of water and the Spirit, we cannot,' as the Truth says, 'enter into the kingdom of heaven' [John 3:5]. The matter of this sacrament is real and natural water."

Pope Julius III, Council of Trent, *On the Sacraments of Baptism and Penance,* Sess. 14, Chap. 2, *ex cathedra*: "But in fact this sacrament [Penance] is seen to differ in many respects from baptism. For, apart from the fact that the matter and form, by which the essence of a sacrament is constituted, are totally distinct, there is certainly no doubt that the minister of baptism need not be a judge, since the Church exercises judgment on no one who has not previously entered it by the gate of baptism. For what have I to do with those who are without (1 Cor. 5:12), says the Apostle. It is otherwise with those of the household of the faith, whom Christ the Lord by the laver of baptism has once made 'members of his own body' (1 Cor. 12:13)."

Pope Paul III, The Council of Trent, Can. 2 on the Sacrament of Baptism, Sess. 7, 1547, *ex cathedra*: "If anyone shall say that real and natural water is not necessary for baptism, and on that account those words of Our Lord Jesus Christ: 'Unless a man be born again of water and the Holy Spirit' [John 3:5], are distorted into some sort of metaphor: let him be anathema."

Pope Paul III, The Council of Trent, Can. 5 on the Sacrament of Baptism, Sess. 7, 1547, *ex cathedra*: "If anyone says that baptism [the sacrament] is optional, that is, not necessary for salvation (cf. Jn. 3:5): let him be anathema."

Pope Paul III, The Council of Trent, *On Original Sin*, Session V, *ex cathedra*: "By one man sin entered into the world, and by sin death... so that in them there may be washed away by regeneration, what they have contracted by generation, 'For unless a man be born again of water and the Holy Ghost, he cannot enter into the kingdom of God [John 3:5]."

Pope Benedict XIV, *Nuper ad nos*, March 16, 1743, Profession of Faith: "Likewise (I profess) that baptism is necessary for salvation, and hence, if there is imminent danger of death, it should be conferred at once and without delay, and that it is valid if conferred with the right matter and form and intention by anyone, and at any time."

Pope Benedict XIV, *Cum Religiosi* (# 1), June 26, 1754: "We could not rejoice, however, when it was subsequently reported to Us that in the course of religious instruction preparatory to Confession and Holy Communion, it was very often found that these people were ignorant of the mysteries of the faith, even those matters which must be known by necessity of means; consequently they were ineligible to partake of the Sacraments."

Pope Benedict XIV, *Cum Religiosi* June 26, 1754 (# 4): "See to it that every minister performs carefully the measures laid down by the holy Council of Trent... that confessors should perform this part of their duty whenever anyone stands at their tribunal who does not know what he must by necessity of means know to be saved..."

Pope Pius IX, *Etsi Multa*, Nov 21, 1873: "Therefore the holy martyr Cyprian, writing about schism, denied to the pseudobishop Novation even the title of Christian, on the grounds that he was cut off and separated from the Church of Christ. "Whoever he is, " he says, "and whatever sort he is, he is not a Christian who is not in the Church of Christ."

Pope St. Pius X, *Acerbo Nimis* (# 2), April 15, 1905: "And so Our Predecessor, Benedict XIV, had just cause to write: 'We declare that a great number of those who are condemned to eternal punishment suffer that everlasting calamity because of ignorance of those mysteries of faith which must be known and believed in order to be numbered among the elect.'"

Pope Pius XII, *Mystici Corporis* (# 22), June 29, 1943: "Actually only those are to be numbered among the members of the Church who have received the laver of regeneration [water baptism] and profess the true faith."

Pope Pius XI, *Quas Primas* (# 15), Dec. 11, 1925: "Indeed this kingdom is presented in the Gospels as such, into which men prepare to enter by doing penance; moreover, they cannot enter it except through faith and baptism, which, although an external rite, yet signifies and effects an interior regeneration."

APPENDIX 3 - ONE BAPTISM NOT THREE

The Nicene-Constantinople Creed, 381, *ex cathedra*: "We confess one baptism for the remission of sins."

Pope St. Celestine I, Council of Ephesus, 431: "Having read these holy phrases and finding ourselves in agreement (for 'there is one Lord, one faith, one baptism' [Eph. 4:5]), we have given glory to God who is the savior of all…"

Pope St. Leo IX, *Congratulamur Vehementer*, April 13, 1053: "I believe that the one true Church is holy, Catholic and apostolic, in which is given one baptism and the true remission of all sins."

Pope Boniface VIII, *Unam Sanctam*, Nov. 18, 1302, *ex cathedra*: "One is my dove, my perfect one… which represents the one mystical body whose head is Christ, of Christ indeed, as God. And in this, 'one Lord, one faith, one baptism' (Eph. 4:5)."

Pope Clement V, Council of Vienne, Decree # 30, 1311-1312, *ex cathedra*: "Since however there is for both regulars and seculars, for superiors and subjects, for exempt and nonexempt, one universal Church, outside of which there is no salvation, for all of whom there is one Lord, one faith, and one baptism…

Pope Pius VI, *Inscrutabile* (# 8), Dec. 25, 1775: "… We exhort and advise you to be all of one mind and in harmony as you strive for the same object, just as the Church has one faith, one baptism, and one spirit."

Pope Leo XII, *Ubi Primum* (# 14), May 5, 1824: "By it we are taught, and by divine faith we hold one Lord, one faith, one baptism, and that no other name under heaven is given to men except the name of Jesus Christ in which we must be saved. This is why we profess that there is no salvation outside the Church."

Pope Pius VIII, *Traditi Humilitati* (# 4), May 24, 1829: "Against these experienced sophists the people must be taught that the profession of the Catholic faith is uniquely true, as the apostle proclaims: one Lord, one faith, one baptism (Eph. 4:5)."

Pope Gregory XVI, *Mirari Vos* (# 13), Aug. 15, 1832: "With the admonition of the apostle that 'there is one God, one faith, one baptism' (Eph. 4:5) may those fear who contrive the notion that the safe harbor of salvation is open to persons of any religion whatever."

Pope Leo XIII, *Graves de communi re* (# 8), Jan. 18, 1901: "Hence the doctrine of the Apostle, who warns us that 'We are one body and spirit called to the one hope in our vocation; one Lord, one faith and one baptism…'"

APPENDIX 4 - ON LAWS AND DISCIPLINES OF THE CHURCH

According to the Catholic Church, she is infallible (without error) in her universal disciplinary laws and practices, and has declared that she cannot issue a practice, which is evil and harmful to the faithful. Examples of the teaching of infallible disciplines from 4 popes and 7 theologians:

Pope Pius VI, *Auctorem Fidei*, 78 (1794): "The prescription of the synod about the order of transacting business in the conferences, in which, after it prefaced 'in every article that which pertains to faith and to essence of religion must be distinguished from that which is proper to discipline,' it adds, 'in this itself (discipline) there is to be distinguished what is necessary or useful to retain the faithful in spirit, from that which is useless or too burdensome for the liberty of the sons of the new Covenant to endure, but more so, from that which is dangerous or harmful, namely, leading to superstition and materialism'; in so far as by the generality of the words it includes and submits to a prescribed examination even the discipline established and approved by the Church, **as if the Church which is ruled by the Spirit of God could have established discipline which is not only useless and burdensome for Christian liberty to endure, but which is even dangerous and harmful and leading to superstition and materialism, - false, rash, scandalous, dangerous, offensive to pious ears, injurious to the Church and to the Spirit of God by whom it is guided, at least erroneous.**" (Denzinger 1578; DS 2678)

Pope Gregory XVI, *Mirari Vos*, 9 (1832): "Furthermore, **the discipline sanctioned by the Church must never be rejected or branded as contrary to certain principles of the natural law. It must never be called crippled, or imperfect or subject to civil authority**. In this discipline the administration of sacred rites, standards of morality, and the reckoning of the Church and her ministers are embraced."

Pope Gregory XVI, *Quo Graviora*, 4-5 (1833): "...[the evil "reformers"] state categorically that there are **many things in the discipline of the Church** in the present day, in its government, and in the form of its external worship which are not suited to the character of our time. **These things, they say, should be changed, as they are harmful for the growth and prosperity of the Catholic religion, before the teaching of faith and morals suffers any harm from it.** Therefore, showing a zeal for religion and showing themselves as an example of piety, they force reforms, conceive of changes, and pretend to renew the Church. **While these men were shamefully straying in their thoughts, they proposed to fall upon the errors condemned by the Church in proposition 78 of the constitution *Auctorem fidei* (published by Our predecessor, Pius VI on August 28, 1794).** They also attacked the pure doctrine which they say they want to keep safe and sound; either they do not understand the situation or craftily pretend not to understand it. While they contend that the entire exterior form of the Church can be changed indiscriminately, do they not subject to change even those items of discipline which have their basis in divine law and which are linked with the doctrine of faith in a close bond? Does not the law of the believer thus produce the law of the doer? Moreover, **do they not try to make the Church human by taking away from the infallible and divine authority, by which divine will it is governed? And does it not produce the same effect to think that the present discipline of the Church rests on failures, obscurities, and other inconveniences of this kind? And to feign that this discipline contains many things which are not useless but which are against the safety of the Catholic religion?** Why is it that private individuals appropriate for themselves the right which is proper only for the pope?"

Pope St. Pius X, *Pascendi Dominici Gregis,* Sept 13, 1907: "Venerable Brethren, the principles from which these doctrines spring have been solemnly condemned by Our predecessor, Pius VI, in his Apostolic Constititution Auctorem fidei."

Pope Pius XII, *Mystici Corporis*, 66 (1943): "Certainly the loving Mother is spotless in the Sacraments, by which she gives birth to and nourishes her children; in the faith which she has always preserved inviolate; in her sacred laws imposed on all; in the evangelical counsels which she recommends; in those heavenly gifts and extraordinary graces through which, with inexhaustible fecundity, she generates hosts of martyrs, virgins and confessors."

Monsignor G. Van Noort, S.T.D. *Dogmatic Theology* 2:91 (1958): "The Church's infallibility extends to....ecclesiastical laws passed for the universal Church for the direction of Christian worship and Christian living....But the Church is infallible in issuing a doctrinal decree as intimated above - and to such an extent that it can never sanction a universal law which would be at odds with faith or morality or would be by its very nature conducive to the injury of souls.... If the Church should make a mistake in the manner alleged when it legislated for the general discipline, it would no longer either be a loyal guardian of revealed doctrine or a trustworthy teacher of the Christian way of life. It would *not be a guardian of revealed doctrine*, for the imposition of a vicious law would be, for all practical purposes, tantamount to an erroneous definition of doctrine; everyone would naturally conclude that what the Church commanded squared with sound doctrine. It would *not be a teacher of the Christian way of life*, for by its laws it would induce corruption into the practice of religious life."

P. Hermann, *Institutiones Theologiae Dogmaticae* (4th ed., Rome: Della Pace, 1908), vol. 1, p. 258: "The Church is infallible in her general discipline. By the term general discipline is understood the laws and practices which belong to the external ordering of the whole Church. Such things would be those which concern either external worship, such as liturgy and rubrics, or the administration of the sacraments. . . . "If she [the Church] were able to prescribe or command or tolerate in her discipline something against faith and morals, or something which tended to the detriment of the Church or to the harm of the faithful, she would turn away from her divine mission, which would be impossible."

A Dorsch, *Institutiones Theologiae Fundamentalis*. Innsbruck: Rauch 1928. 2:409: "The Church is also rightfully held to be infallible in her disciplinary decrees....By disciplinary decrees are understood all those things which pertain to the ruling of the Church,, insofar as it is distinguished from the magisterium. Referred to here, then, are ecclesiastical laws which the Church laid down for the Universal Church in order to regulate divine worship or to direct the Christian life."

R.M. Schultes *De Ecclesia Catholica*. Paris: Lethielleux 1931. 314-7: "*The infallibility of the Church in Enacting Disciplinary Laws*. Disciplinary laws are defined as 'ecclesiastical laws laid down to direct Christian life and worship'..... The question of whether the Church is infallible in establishing a disciplinary law concerns the substance of universal disciplinary laws - that is, whether such laws can be contrary to a teaching of faith or morals, and so work to the spiritual harm of the faithful....*Thesis. The Church, in establishing universal laws, is infallible as regards their substance*. The Church is infallible in matters of faith and morals. Through disciplinary laws, the Church teaches about matters of faith and morals, not doctrinally or theoretically, put practically and effectively. A disciplinary law therefore involves a doctrinal judgement.... The reason, therefore, and foundation for the Church's infallibility in her general discipline is the intimate connection between truths of faith or morals and disciplinary laws. The principal matter of disciplinary laws is as follows:a)worship...."

Valentino Zubizarreta *Theologia Dogmatico-Scholastica*. 4th ed. Vitoria: El Carmen 1948. 1:486: " *Corollary II*. In establishing disciplinary laws for the universal Church, the Church is likewise infallible, in such a way that she would never legislate something which would contradict true faith or good morals. Church discipline is defined as 'that legislation or collection of laws which direct men how to worship God rightly and how to live a good Christian life.'.... *Proof of the Corollary*. It has been shown above that the Church enjoys infallibility in those things which concern faith and morals, or which are necessarily required for their preservation. Disciplinary laws, prescribed for the universal Church in order to worship God and rightly promote a good Christian life, are implicitly revealed in matters of morals, and are necessary to preserve faith and good morals. Therefore, the Corollary is proved."

Serapius Iragui, *Manuale Theologiae Dogmaticae*. Madrid: Ediciones Stadium 1959. 1:436, 447: "Outside those truths revealed in themselves, the object of the magisterium's infallibility includes other truths which, while not revealed, are nevertheless necessary to integrally preserve the deposit of the faith, correctly explain it, and effectively define it.... D) *Disciplinary Decrees*. These decrees are universal ecclesiastical laws which govern man's Christian life and divine worship. Even though the faculty of establishing laws pertains to the power of jurisdiction, nevertheless the power of the magisterium is considered in these laws under another special aspect, insofar as there must be nothing in these laws opposed to the natural or positive law. In this respect, we say that the judgement of the Church is infallible.... 1°) This is required by the nature and purpose of infallibility, for the infallible Church must lead her subjects to sanctification through a correct exposition of doctrine. Indeed, if the Church in her universally binding decrees would impose false doctrine, by that very fact men would be turned away from salvation, and the very nature of the true Church would be placed in peril. All this, however, is repugnant to the prerogative of infallibility with which Christ endowed His Church. Therefore, when the Church establishes disciplinary laws, she must be infallible."

Joachim Salaverri, *Sacrae Theologiae Summa*. 5th ed. Madrid: BAC 1962. 1:722,723: "3) Regarding disciplinary decrees in general which are by their purpose [*finaliter*] connected with things which God has revealed. A. The purpose of the infallible Magisterium requires infallibility for decrees of this kind.... Specifically, that the Church claims infallibility for herself in liturgical decrees is established by the law of the Councils of Constance and Trent solemnly enacted regarding Eucharistic Communion under one species. This can also be abundantly proved from other decrees, by which the Council of Trent solemnly confirmed the rites and ceremonies used in the administration of the sacraments and the celebration of the Mass."

APPENDIX 5 – BAPTISM OF DESIRE AND BLOOD BY THE SAINTS AND DOCTORS OF THE CHURCH

Baptism of Desire or Blood is the belief of nearly all the Church Fathers. It does not prove the doctrine but it proves that it is the constant teaching of the Church and cannot be condemned as heresy.

Justin Martyr (100-martyred 165)

First Apology 46 [A.D. 151]:

"We have been taught that Christ is the first-begotten of God, and we have declared him to be the Logos of which all mankind partakes [John 1:9]. Those, therefore, who lived according to reason [Greek, logos] were really Christians, even though they were thought to be atheists, such as, among the Greeks, Socrates, Heraclitus, and others like them. . . . Those who lived before Christ but did not live according to reason [logos] were wicked men, and enemies of Christ, and murderers of those who did live according to reason [logos], whereas those who lived then or who live now according to reason [logos] are Christians. Such as these can be confident and unafraid."

St. Cyprian (martyred in 257)

Enchiridion Patristicum (paragraph 1328):

"Some people, as if by human argument they could rob of its truth the teaching of the Gospel, present us with the case of catechumens, demanding whether, if one of these, before he was baptized in the church, were captured and killed in the confession of his belief, he would forfeit his hope of salvation and the reward of his confession because he had not previously been born again by water. Men of this kind, who laud and abet heretics, are well aware that those catechumens who first hold inviolate the faith and truth of the Church and advance, with full and sincere knowledge of God the Father and Christ and the Holy Ghost, to fight off the devil from the Divine battlements are certainly not thereupon deprived of the sacrament of baptism seeing that they have been baptized with the greatest and most glorious baptism of blood, concerning which Our Lord said that He had another baptism wherewith to be baptized (Luke 12:50). The same Lord, however, affirms in the gospel that those who are baptized by their own blood and sanctified by their sufferings, are consummated and receive the grace of the Divine promise. This is implied by His words when he spoke to the thief who believed in and confessed His passion, promising that he would be with him in paradise."

Again, St. Cyprian

To Jubaianus (254):

"Catechumens who suffer martyrdom before they have received Baptism with water are not deprived of the Sacrament of Baptism. Rather, they are baptized with the most glorious and greatest Baptism of Blood..."Jurgens, The Faith of the Early Fathers, Vol. 1: 598

St. Augustine (354-430 great Doctor of the Church)

City of God (397)

"Those also who die for the confession of Christ without having received the laver of regeneration are released thereby from their sins just as much as if they had been cleansed by the sacred spring of baptism. For He who said, 'Unless a man be born again of water and the Holy Ghost, he cannot enter into the kingdom of God,' (John 3:5) by another statement made exceptions to this when He said no less comprehensively: 'Everyone... that shall confess me before men, I will confess before my Father who is in Heaven.' (Matthew 10:32)."

St. Cyril of Jerusalem (died in 386 Doctor of the Church)

"If anyone does not receive baptism, he does not have salvation, excepting only martyrs who gain the kingdom even without water."

St. Gregory Nazianzen (died 389 Doctor of the Church)

"…**let us speak about the different kinds of Baptism, that we may come out thence purified.** Moses baptized Leviticus xi but it was in water, and before that in the cloud and in the sea. I Corinthians 10:2 This was typical as Paul says; the Sea of the water, and the Cloud of the Spirit; the Manna, of the Bread of Life; the Drink, of the Divine Drink. John also baptized; but this was not like the baptism of the Jews, for it was not only in water, but also unto repentance. Still it was not wholly spiritual, for he does not add And in the Spirit. Jesus also baptized, but in the Spirit. This is the perfect Baptism. And how is He not God, if I may digress a little, by whom you too are made God? **I know also a Fourth Baptism**— that by Martyrdom and blood, which also Christ himself underwent:— and this one is far more august than all the others, inasmuch as it cannot be defiled by after-stains. **Yes, and I know of a Fifth also**, which is that of tears, and is much more laborious, received by him who washes his bed every night and his couch with tears; whose bruises stink through his wickedness; and who goes mourning and of a sad countenance; who imitates the repentance of Manasseh Ninevites Jonah 3:7-10 upon which God had mercy; who utters the words of the Publican in the Temple, and is justified rather than the stiff-necked Pharisee; Luke 18:13 who like the Canaanite woman bends down and asks for mercy and crumbs, the food of a dog that is very hungry. Matthew 15:27" Catholic Encyclopedia (1908)

St. John Chrysostom (died 407 Doctor of the Church)

Panegyric on St. Lucianus:

"Do not be surprised that I should equate martyrdom with baptism; for here too the spirit blows with much fruitfulness, and a marvellous and astonishing remission of sins and cleansing of the soul is effected; and just as those who are baptized by water, so, too, those who suffer martyrdom are cleansed with their own blood."

St. Fulgentius (died early 500's):

"From the time when Our Saviour said 'Unless a man be born again of water and the Holy Ghost, he cannot enter into the kingdom of

God,' without the sacrament of baptism, apart from those who pour forth their blood for Christ in the Catholic Church without baptism, no one can receive the kingdom of Heaven, nor eternal life."

St. Alban and his fellow martyr: SEE OBJECTION # 28

The Venerable Bede (673-735 Doctor of the Church) tells us in the Ecclesiastical History of the Church of the English Nation the story of an early English Martyr. The story is well summarized by Dom Gueranger (who St. Theresa of Lisieaux considered to be a saint) in his Liturgical Year:

"When the mandates of the emperors Diocletian and Maximian were raging against the Christians, Alban, as yet a pagan, received into his house a certain priest fleeing from persecution. Now, when he [Alban] beheld how this priest persevered day and night in constant watching and prayer, he was suddenly touched by divine grace, so that he was fain to imitate the example of his faith and piety; and being instructed by degrees, through his salutary exhortations, forsaking the darkness of idolatry, he with his whole heart became a Christian."

"The persecutors, being in search of this cleric, came to Alban's house, whereupon, disguised in the cleric's apparel - namely, in the caracalla - he presented himself to the soldiers in the place of his master and guest; by them he was bound with things, and led off to the judge. This latter finding himself thus deceived, ordered that the holy confessor of God should be beaten by the executioners; and, perceiving at last that he could neither overcome him by torments, nor win him over from the worship of the Christian religion, he commanded his head to be struck off."

"Alban having reached the brow of the neighboring hill, the executioner who was to dispatch him, admonished by a divine inspiration, casting away his sword, threw himself at the saint's feet, desiring to die either with the martyr, or instead of him. Alban, being at once beheaded, received the crown of life, which God hath promised to them that love him."

"The soldier who had refused to strike him, was likewise beheaded: concerning whom it is quite certain that, albeit he was not washed in the baptismal font, still was he made clean in the laver of his own blood and so made worthy of entering into the kingdom of heaven. Alban suffered at Verulam, on the tenths of the Kalends of July. And the judge, astonished at the novelty of so many heavenly miracles, ordered the persecution to cease immediately, beginning to honor the death of the saints [only St. Alban and the soldier had been executed], by which [death] he had before thought that they might be diverted from the Christian faith."

As Martin Gwynne points out, this last paragraph is taken verbatum from the writings of Bede, and Bede is a Doctor of the Church. Moreover, St. Alban, who died on June 22 in the year 303, is considered to be the proto-martyr of the English Church. SEE OBJECTION 28

St. John Damascene (676-died late 700's Doctor of the Church)

"These things were well understood by our holy and inspired fathers thus they strove, **after Holy Baptism**, to keep... spotless and undefiled. Whence some of them also thought fit to receive **another** Baptism: I mean that which is by blood and martyrdom." Barlam and Josaphat, Woodward & Heineman, trans., pp. 169 171.

St. Bernard (died 1153 great Doctor of the Church)

Tractatus de baptismo, II, 8, c. 1130:

"So, believe me, it would be difficult to turn me aside from these two pillars – I mean Augustine and Ambrose. I confess that, **whether in error or knowledge**, I am with them; **for I believe that a man can be saved by faith alone, provided he desires to receive the sacrament,** in a case where death overtakes the fulfillment of his religious desire, or some other invincible power stands in his way." Quoted by Fr. Jean Marc Rulleau, Baptism of Desire, p. 37.

St. Thomas Aquinas (1226-1274 great Doctor of the Church)

Article I, Part III, Q 68:
"7 answer that, the sacrament of Baptism may be wanting to someone in two ways. First, both in reality and in desire; as is the

case with those who neither are baptized, nor wished to be baptized: which clearly indicates contempt of the sacrament, in regard to those who have the use of the free-will. Consequently those to whom Baptism is wanting thus, cannot obtain salvation: since neither sacramentally nor mentally are they incorporated in Christ, through whom alone can salvation be obtained.

"Secondly, the sacrament of Baptism may be wanting to anyone in reality but not in desire: for instance, when a man wishes to be baptized, but by some ill-chance he is forestalled by death before receiving Baptism. And such a man can obtain salvation without being actually baptized, on account of his desire for Baptism, which desire is the outcome of faith that worketh by charity, whereby God, Whose power is not tied to visible sacraments, sanctifies man inwardly. Hence Ambrose says of Valentinian, who died while yet a catechumen: 'I lost him whom I was to regenerate: but he did not lose the grace he prayed for.'

Again, St. Thomas Aquinas

Summa, Part III, Question 66, Eleventh Article
"As stated in question 62, fifth article, baptism of water has its efficacy from Christ's Passion, to which a man is conformed by baptism, and also from the Holy Ghost as first cause. Now although the effect depends on the first cause, the cause far surpasses the effect, nor does it depend on it. consequently, a man may, without baptism of water, receive the sacramental effect from Christ's Passion, in so far as he is conformed to Christ by suffering for Him. Hence it is written (Apocalypse 7:14): 'these are they who are come out of great tribulation, and have washed their robes and made them white in the blood of the Lamb.' In like manner a man receives the effect of baptism by the power of the Holy Ghost, not only without baptism of water, but also without baptism of blood: forasmuch as his heart is moved by the Holy Ghost to believe in and love God and to repent of his sins: wherefore this is also called the baptism of repentance. Of this it is written (Isaias 4:4): 'If the Lord shall wash away the filth of the daughters of Sion, and shall wash away the blood of Jerusalem out of the midst thereof, by the spirit of judgement, and by the spirit of burning.' Thus, therefore, each of these other baptisms is called baptism, forasmuch as it takes the place of baptism."

St. Thomas completes this article by quoting the passage from St. Augustine He then moves on to the next question (66):

"Augustine [Ad Fortunatum], speaking of the comparison between baptisms says: 'the newly baptized confesses his faith in the presence of the priest; the martyr in the presence of the persecutor. The former is sprinkled with water, after he has confessed; the latter with his blood. The former receives the Holy Ghost by the imposition of the bishop's hands; the latter is made the temple of the Holy Ghost.'"

"As stated above (article 11), the shedding of blood for Christ's sake, and the inward operation of the Holy Ghost, are called baptisms, in so far as they produce the effect of the baptism of water. Now the baptism of water derives its efficacy from the Holy Ghost, as already stated. These two causes act in each of these three baptisms; most excellently, however, in the baptism of blood. For Christ's Passion acts in the baptism of water by way of desire; but in the baptism of blood by way of imitating the (Divine) act. In like manner, too, the power of the Holy Ghost acts in the baptism of water through a certain hidden power; in the baptism of repentance by moving the heart; but in the baptism of blood by the highest degree of fervor of dilection and love, according to John 15:13 'Greater love then this no man hath that a man lay down his life for his friends.'"

Again, St. Thomas Aquinas

Commentary on the Gospel of St. John (section 444):

"Two questions arise here. First, if no one enters the kingdom of God unless he is born again of water, and if the fathers of old were not born again of water (because they were not baptized), then they have not entered the kingdom of God. Secondly, since baptism is of three kinds, that is, of water, of desire and of blood, and many have been baptized in the latter two ways (who we say have entered the kingdom of God immediately, even though they were not born again of water), it does not seem to be true to say that unless one is born again of water and the Holy Spirit, he cannot enter the kingdom of God. The answer to the first is that rebirth or regeneration from water and the holy spirit takes place in two ways: in truth and in symbol. Now the fathers of old, although they were not reborn with a true rebirth, were nevertheless reborn with a symbolic rebirth, because they always had a sense perceptible sign in which true rebirth was prefigured. So according to this, thus reborn, they did enter the kingdom of God, after the ransom was paid. The answer to the second is that those who are reborn by a baptism of blood and fire, although they do not have regeneration in deed, they do have it in desire. Otherwise neither would the baptism of blood mean anything nor could there be a baptism of the Spirit. Consequently, in order than man may enter the kingdom of heaven, it is necessary that there baptism of water in deed, as is the case of all baptized persons, or in desire, as in the case of the martyrs and catechumens, who are prevented by death from fulfilling their desire, or in symbol as in the case of the fathers of old."

St. Robert Bellarmine (1542-1621 great Doctor of the Church)

Liber II, Caput XXX:

"Boni Cathecumeni sunt de Ecclesia, interna unione tantum, non autem externa." (Good catechumens are of the Church, by internal union only, not however, by external union.)

St. Alphonsus Liguori (1696-1775 great Doctor of the Church): Moral Theology, Bk. 6, nn. 95-7. Concerning Baptism:

Baptism, therefore, coming from a Greek word that means ablution or immersion in water, is distinguished into Baptism of water *["fluminis"]*, of desire [*"flaminis"* = wind] and of blood.

We shall speak below of Baptism of water, which was very probably instituted before the passion of Christ the Lord, when Christ was baptised by John. But Baptism of desire is perfect conversion to God by contrition or love of God above all things accompanied by an explicit or implicit desire for true Baptism of water, the place of which it takes as to the remission of guilt, but not as to the impression of the [baptismal] character or as to the removal of all debt of punishment. It is called "of wind" ["flaminis"] because it takes place by the impulse of the Holy Ghost who is called a wind ["flamen"]. Now it is de fide that men are also saved by Baptism of desire, by virtue of the Canon Apostolicam, "de presbytero non baptizato" and of the Council of Trent, session 6, Chapter 4 where it is said that no one can be saved "without the laver of regeneration or the desire for it".

Baptism of blood is the shedding of one's blood, i.e. death, suffered for the Faith or for some other Christian virtue. Now this Baptism is comparable to true Baptism because, like true Baptism, it remits both guilt and punishment as it were ex opere operato. I say as it were because martyrdom does not act by as strict a causality ["non ita stricte"] as the sacraments, but by a certain privilege on account of its resemblance to the passion of Christ. Hence martyrdom avails also for infants seeing that the Church venerates the Holy Innocents as true martyrs. That is why Suarez rightly teaches that the opposing view [i.e. the view that infants are not able to benefit from Baptism of blood – translator] is at least temerarious. In adults, however, acceptance of martyrdom is required, at least habitually from a supernatural motive.

It is clear that martyrdom is not a sacrament, because it is not an action instituted by Christ, and for the same reason neither was the Baptism of John

Again, St. Alphonsus Liquori

"Truly Baptism of Blood is the pouring forth of blood, or undergone for the sake of the faith, or for some other Christian virtue; as teaches St. Thomas, Viva; Croix along with Aversa and Gobet, etc. This is equivalent to real baptism because [it acts] as if it were ex operato and like Baptism remits both sin and punishment. It is said to be quasi - as if, because martyrdom is not strictly speaking like a sacrament, but because those privileged in this way imitate the Passion of Christ as says Bellarmin, Suarez, Sotus, Cajetane, etc., along with Croix; and in a firm manner, Petrocorensis."

"Therefore martyrdom is efficacious, even in infants, as is shown by the Holy Innocents which are indeed considered true martyrs. This is clearly taught by Suarez along with Croix and to oppose such an opinion is indeed temerarious. In adults it is necessary that martyrdom be at least habitually accepted from supernatural motives as Coninck, Cajetan, Suarez, Bonacina and Croix etc. teach. ...."

"Not in passing that such was also the teaching of Coninck, Cajetan, Suarez Bonacina and Croix."

A Private Revelation of the Great Saint Catherine of Sienna

St. Catherine of Sienna (1347-1380)

Christ addressed the issue of Baptism in response to her question in the following terms:

"I wished thee to see the secret of the Heart, showing it to thee open, so that tyou mightest see how much more I loved than I could show thee by finite pain. I poured from it Blood and Water, to show thee the baptism of water which is received in virtue of the Blood. I also showed the baptism of love in two ways, first in those who are baptized in their blood shed for Me which has virtue through My Blood, even if they have not been able to have Holy Baptism, and also those who are baptized in fire, not being able to have Holy Baptism, but desiring it with the affection of love. There is no baptism of desire without the Blood, because Blood is steeped in and kneaded with the fire of Divine charity, because through love was it shed. There is yet another way by which the soul receives the baptism of Blood, speaking, as it were, under a figure, and this way the Divine charity provided, knowing the infirmity and fragility of an, through which he offends, not that he is obliged, through his fragility and infirmity, to commit sin, unless he wish to do so; by falling, as he will, into the guild of mortal sin, by which he loses the grace which he drew from Holy Baptism in virtue of the Blood, it was necessary to leave a continual baptism of blood. This the Divine charity provided in the Sacrament of Holy Confession, the soul receiving the Baptism of blood, with contrition of heart, confessing, when able, to My ministers, who hold the keys of the Blood, sprinkling It, in absolution, upon the face of the soul. But if the soul is unable to confess, contrition of heart is sufficient for this baptism, the hand of My clemency giving you the fruit of this precious Blood... Thou seest then that these Baptisms, which you should all receive until the last moment, are continual, and though My works, that is the pains of the Cross were finite, the fruit of them which you receive in Baptism, through Me, are infinite..."

Historical examples

Drawing from the Bollandists who are the official hagiorapher of the Church. We take two examples drawn from Les Petits Bollandistes:

The first is the story of the brother martyrs Saints Donatien and Rogatien, who were martyred during the reign of Maximien about the year 287 and who are the patron saints of the city of Nantes in France.

"There was a young man in Nantes called Donatien. Born into an illustrious family, he was even more illustrious for his faith.... He had received baptism, and fortifies by the holy mysteries, he publicly proclaimed the triumph of Jesus Christ and spread the divine wheat that had been so fruitful in him own heart, in the hearts of the Gentiles around him."

"He gained his elder brother Rogatien who was still an idolator to the Christian faith at a time of great peril, for it was a period when the profession of Christianity was proscribed. But such considerations did not deter Rogatien from adhering to the truth and committing himself to following Jesus Christ, even unto death. In order to have the strength to undertake this dangerous combat, he sought out the sacrament of baptism with great ardor, but in the absence of a priest (sacerdotis absentia fugitiva) - for the priests had been forced to flee the land - he could only be baptized in his own blood.

Rogatien and his brother were placed in the same goal and Rogatien had only one sorrow - that he had not receive baptism. Continuing the story as provided by the Bollandists:

"But the faith which he had in God led him to hope that the kiss of his brother would take the place of the sacred bath [baptism]. Donatien, informed of the sorrow of his brother, made the following prayer to God: 'Lord Jesus Christ, with whom desires have the same merit as works, when it is absolutely impossible to fulfill the wishes of someone who is completely devoted to you, as is the case with your servant Rogatien, grant if the judge persists in his obstinacy, that his pure faith may take the place of baptism, and that his blood may become the sacred oils."

The following morning both brothers were slain, and "Donatien, having gained his brother to Jesus Christ, had the consolation of seeing him respond with dignity to the graces of his vocation; Rogatien, baptized in his own blood, showed himself in no way inferior to his brother, and the two achieved an illustrious victory and were united in the happy flock that is never to be separated from the immortal Lamb, the author and consummator of their beatitude." There are many churches in the districts around Nantes dedicated to these two saints.

Taken from Book Two, Part Six of De Sacramentis by Hugh of St. Victor, (13th Century)

Some either through curiosity or zeal are accustomed to inquire whether anyone after the enjoining and proclaiming of the sacrament of baptism can be saved, unless he actually receives the sacrament of baptism itself. For the reasons seem to be manifest and they have many authorities, (if, however, they are said to have authorities, who do not understand); first, because it is said: "Unless a man be born again of the water and the Holy Ghost, he cannot enter into the kingdom of God," (Cf. John 3, 5), and again: "He that believeth and is baptized, shall be saved," (Mark 16, 16). There are many such passages which seem, as it were, to affirm that by no means can he be saved who has not had this sacrament, whatever he may have besides this sacrament. If he should have perfect faith, if hope, if he should have charity, even if he should have a contrite and humble heart which God does not despise, true repentance for the past, firm purpose for the future, whatever he may have, he will not be able to be saved, if he does not have this. All this seems so to them on account of what is written: "Unless a man be born again of the water and the Holy Ghost, he cannot enter into the kingdom of God," (Cf. John 3, 5).

Yet if someone would ask; what has happened to those who, after shedding blood for Christ, departed this life without the sacrament of water, they dare not say that men of this kind are not saved. And, although one cannot show that this is written in what is mentioned above, yet they dare not say that, because it is not written there, it is to be denied. For he who said: "Unless a man be born again of the water and the Holy Ghost," did not add: "or by pouring forth his blood instead of water, " and yet this is true, although it is not written here. For if he is saved who received water on account of God, why is he not saved much more who sheds blood on account of God? For it is more to give blood than to receive water. Moreover, what some say is clearly silly, that those who shed blood are saved because with blood they also shed water in the very water which they shed they receive baptism. For if those who are killed are said to have been baptized on account of the moisture of water which drips from their wounds together with the corruption of blood, then those who are suffocated or drowned or are killed by some other kind of death where blood is not shed have not been baptized in their blood and have died for Christ in vain, because they did not shed the moisture of the water which they had within their body. Who would say this? So, he is baptized in blood who dies for Christ, who, even if he does not shed blood from the wound, gives life which is more precious than blood. For he could shed blood and, if he did not give life, shedding blood would be less than giving life. Therefore, he sheds blood well who lays down his life for Christ, and he has his baptism in the virtue of the sacrament, without which to have received the sacrament itself, as it were, is of no benefit. So where this is the case, to be unable to have the sacrament does no harm.

Thus, it is true, although it is not said there, that he who dies for Christ is baptized in Christ. Thus, they say, it is true, although it is not said there, and it is true because it is said elsewhere, even if it is not said there. For He who said: "Unless a man be born again of the water and the Holy Ghost, he cannot enter into the Kingdom of God," the same also said elsewhere: "He who shall confess me before men, I will also confess him before my Father," (Cf. Matt.10, 32). And so what is not said there, is nevertheless to be understood although it is not said, since it is said elsewhere. Behold therefore why they say it. They say that what is not said is to be understood where it is not said, because it is said elsewhere. If, therefore, this is to be understood in this place where it is not said, since it is said elsewhere: "He who believeth in me, shall not die forever," (Cf. John 11, 26). Likewise He who said: "Unless a man be born again of the water and the Holy

Ghost, he cannot enter into the Kingdom of God, " He himself said: "He who believeth in me, shall not die for ever." therefore, either deny faith or concede salvation. What does it seem to you? Where there is faith, where there is hope, where there is charity, finally, where there is the full and perfect virtue of the sacrament, there is no salvation because the sacrament alone is not and it is not, because it cannot be possessed. "He that believeth," He said, "and is baptized, shall be saved," (Mark 16, 16). Therefore behold there is no doubt but that where there is faith and is baptism, there is salvation.

And what follows? "But he that believeth shall not be condemned," (Cf. Mark 16, 16). Why did He wish to speak thus? Why did He not say: "He that believeth not and is not baptized, shall be condemned," just as He had said: "He that believeth and is baptized, shall be saved?" Why, unless because it is of the will to believe and because he who wishes to believe cannot lack faith. And so in him who does not believe, an evil will is always shown, where there can be no necessity which may be put forth as an excuse. Now to be baptized can be in the will, even when it is not possibility, and on this account justly is good will with the with the devotion of its faith not to be despised, although in a moment of necessity he is prevented from receiving that sacrament of water which is external. Do you wish to know more fully whether or not this reason is proven elsewhere by more manifest authority, although even those authorities which we have mentioned above seem so manifest that there can be no doubt about the truth of them?

Listen to something more, if by chance this matter about which you should not be in doubt can be shown you more clearly. Blessed Augustine in his book, "On the One Baptism," speaks as follows: again and again as I consider it, I find that not only suffering for the name of Christ can fulfill what was lacking to baptism but also faith and conversion of heart, if perhaps assistance could not be rendered for the celebration of the mystery of baptism in straitened circumstances. You see that he clearly testifies that faith and conversion of heart can suffice for the salvation of good will where it happens that the visible sacrament of water of necessity cannot be had. But lest perhaps you think that he contradicted himself, since afterwards in the Book of Retractions he disapproved of the example of the thief which he had assumed to establish this opinion where he had said that the shedding of blood or faith and change of heart could fulfill the place of baptism, saying: "In the fourth book, when I said that suffering could take the place of baptism, I did not furnish a sufficiently fitting example in that of the thief about whom there is some doubt as to whether he was baptized," you should consider that in this place he only corrected an example which he had offered to prove his opinion; he did not reject his opinion. But if you think that that opinion is to be rejected, because the example is corrected, then what he had said is false, that the shedding of blood can take the place of baptism, since the example itself was furnished to prove that. For he does not say: "When I said that faith could have the place of baptism," but he says: "When I said that suffering could have the place of baptism," although he had placed both in the one opinion. If, therefore, regarding what he said, that suffering can have the place of baptism, an example has been furnished, since it is established that it is true without any ambiguity, it is clear that the example was afterwards corrected by the opinion was not rejected.

You should, therefore, either confess that true faith and confession of the heart can fulfill the place of baptism in the moment of necessity or show how true faith and unfeigned charity can be possessed where there is no salvation. Unless perhaps you wish to say that no one can have true faith and true charity, who is not to have the visible sacrament of water. Yet by what reason or by what authority you prove this I do not know. We meanwhile do not ask whether anyone who is not to receive the sacrament of baptism can have these, since this alone as far as this matter is concerned is certain: if there were anyone who had these even without the visible sacrament of water he could not perish. There are many other things which could have been brought up to prove this, but what we have set forth above in the treatment of the sacraments to prove this point we by no means think needs reconsideration.

APPENDIX 6 - THE FEWNESS OF THE SAVED

Christ was clear that most people don't make it to heaven, despite the fact that most people think to the contrary. One of the great deceptions from the devil is that God is so merciful that He will not send people to hell. The fact is people send themselves there because they don't truly love God in word and deed. St. Theresa of Avila said most priests go to hell. St. Chrysostom said the road to hell is paved with the skulls of bishops. I submit that many if not most of the popes probably even went to hell because of their thirst for power, greed, or luxury. If you want to be among the few that are saved, then you must live like the very few that are saved. Below are those statements found in the Holy Bible and the great men of the Church that teach the fewness of the saved.

First, the Holy Scriptures:

New Testament:

Lord, are there few that are saved? But he said to them: Strive to enter by the narrow gate; for many, I tell you, shall seek to enter, and shall not be able. **St. Luke 13:23-24**

Enter ye in at the narrow gate; for wide is the gate and broad is the way that leads to destruction, and many there are who go in thereat. How narrow is the gate and how strait is the way that leads to life, and few there are that find it! **St. Matthew 7:13-14**

Bind his hands and feet, and cast him into exterior darkness; there shall be weeping and gnashing of teeth. For many are called but few are chosen. **St. Matthew 22:13-14**

If the just man shall scarcely be saved, where shall the ungodly man and the sinner appear? **I St. Peter 4:18**

Old Testament:

And they [...] shall be so few that they shall easily be counted, and a child shall write them down. **Isaias 10:19**

And it shall be as when a man gathers in the harvest which remains. [...] And the fruit thereof that shall be left shall be as a single cluster of grapes; and as the shaking of the olive tree: two or three berries on the top of the bough, of four or five on the top of the tree, says the Lord, the God of Israel. **Isaias 17:5-6**

For thus it shall be in the midst of the earth, in the midst of the people, as though a few olives that remain should be shaken out of the olive tree, or grapes when the vintage is ended. **Isaias 24:13**

The holy man is perished from off the earth, and there is no one upright amongst men: they all lie in wait for blood, every one. [...] He who is best among them is like a brier, and he who is righteous as the thorn. **Micheas 7:2,4**

The Popes who are Saints:

Pope St. Gregory the Great (540-604): There are many who arrive at the faith, but few who are led into the heavenly kingdom. Behold how many are gathered here for today's Feast-Day: we fill the church from wall to wall. Yet who knows how few they are who shall be numbered in that chosen company of the Elect? Gregory: "On the Gospels," Homily 19. Sunday Sermons of the Great Fathers, trans. and ed., Fr. M. F. Toal, Chicago: Regnery Co., 1955, I:382

The more the wicked abound, so much the more must we suffer with them in patience; for on the threshing floor few are the grains carried into the barns, but high are the piles of chaff burned with fire. Gregory: Homily 38

The Ark, which in the midst of the Flood was a symbol of the Church, was wide below and narrow above; and, at the summit, measured only a single cubit. [...] It was wide where the animals were, narrow where men lived: for the Holy Church is indeed wide in the number of those who are carnal-minded, narrow in the number of those who are spiritual. Gregory: Homily 38:8

They who are to be saved as Saints, and wish to be saved as imperfect souls, shall not be saved. Gregory: Dignities and Duties of the Priest, 97

Pope St. Pius X (1835-1914): Oh, Jesus, Divine Redeemer of souls, behold how great is the multitude of those who still sleep in the darkness of error! Reckon up the number of those who stray to the edge of the precipice. Consider the throngs of the poor, the hungry, the ignorant, and the feeble who groan in their abandoned condition. Oh Lord, our sins darken our understanding, and hide from us the blessing of loving Thee as Thou dost merit. Enlighten our minds with a ray of Thy divine light. Thou art the Friend, the Redeemer, and the Father of the one who turns penitent to Thy Sacred Heart. Amen. Raccolta, Boston: Benzinger Bros., 1957, 659

Saints who are Doctors of the Church

St. Jerome (347-420): So that you will better appreciate the meaning of Our Lord's words, and perceive more clearly how few the Elect are, note that Christ did not say that those who walked in the path to Heaven are few in number, but that there were few who found that narrow way. It is as though the Saviour intended to say: The path leading to Heaven is so narrow and so rough, so overgrown, so dark and difficult to discern, that there are many who never find it their whole life long. And those who do find it are constantly exposed to the danger of deviating from it, of mistaking their way, and unwittingly wandering away from it, because it is so irregular and overgrown. Jerome: "Commentary on Matthew...Many begin well, but there are few who persevere. "Commentary on Matthew"

St. John Chrysostom (347-407): What do you think? How many of the inhabitants of this city may perhaps be saved? What I am about to tell you is very terrible, yet I will not conceal it from you. Out of this thickly populated city with its thousands of inhabitants not one hundred people will be saved. I even doubt whether there will be as many as that! John: "To the People of Antioch", Homily 40 Quercy "Redemption and Grace", ch.3, Denzinger 318

St. Augustine (354-430): Take care not to resemble the multitude whose knowledge of God's will only condemns them to more severe punishment.

It is certain that few are saved. Sermon 111; also (Against Cresconius)

If you wish to imitate the multitude, then you shall not be among the few who shall enter in by the narrow gate. Sermon 224:1

The Lord called the world a "field" and all the faithful who draw near to him "wheat." All through the field, and around the threshing-floor, there is both wheat and chaff. But the greater part is chaff; the lesser part is wheat, for which is prepared a barn not a fire. [...] The good also are many, but in comparison with the wicked the good are few. Many are the grains of wheat, but compared with the chaff, the grains are few. (Against Cresconius)

St. Anselm (1033-1109): If thou wouldst be certain of being in the number of the elect, strive to be one of the few, not of the many. And if thou wouldst be quite sure of thy salvation, strive to be among the fewest of the few... Do not follow the great majority of mankind, but follow those who enter upon the narrow way, who renounce the world, who give themselves to prayer, and who never relax their efforts by day or by night, that they may attain everlasting blessedness. Fr. Martin Von Cochem, The Four Last Things, p. 221. Anselm, Sunday Sermons of the Great Fathers

St. Thomas Aquinas (1225-1274): There are a select few who are saved. Summa Theologica I, Qu.23, art.7, ad 3. Those who are saved are in the minority. Summa Theologica I q.23, art.8, ad.3

St. Alphonsus Maria Liquori (1696-1787): The greater number of men still say to God: Lord we will not serve Thee; we would rather be slaves of the devil, and condemned to Hell, than be Thy servants. Alas! The greatest number, my Jesus - we may say nearly all - not only do not love Thee, but offend Thee and despise Thee. How many countries there are in which there are scarcely any Catholics, and all the rest either infidels or heretics! And all of them are certainly on the way to being lost. The Incarnation, Birth and Infancy of Jesus Christ, 292.

The greater part of men choose to be damned rather than to love Almighty God. The Way of Salvation and Perfection, 311

All infidels and heretics are surely on the way to being lost. What an obligation we owe God! for causing us to be born not only after the coming of Jesus Christ, but also in countries where the true faith reigns! I thank Thee, O Lord, for this. Woe to me if, after so many transgressions, it had been my fate to live in the midst of infidels or heretics! The Incarnation, Birth and Infancy, 291-2

We owe God a deep regret of gratitude for the purely gratuitous gift of the true faith with which he has favoured us. How many are the infidels, heretics and schismatics who do not enjoy comparable happiness? The earth is full of them and they are all lost! Instructions on the Commandments and Sacraments, 66, no. 19

What is the number of those who love Thee, O God? How few they are! The Elect are much fewer than the damned! Alas! The greater portion of mankind lives in sin unto the devil, and not unto Jesus Christ. O Saviour of the world, I thank Thee for having called and permitted us to live in the true faith which the Holy Roman Catholic Church teaches. [...] But alas, O my Jesus! How small is the number of those who live in this holy faith! Oh, God! The greater number of men lie buried in the darkness of infidelity and heresy. Thou hast humbled Thyself to death, to the death of the cross, for the salvation of men, and these ungrateful men are unwilling even to know Thee. Ah, I pray Thee, O omnipotent God, O sovereign and infinite Good, make all men know and love Thee! On the Council of Trent

St. Teresa, as the Roman Rota attests, never fell into any mortal sin; but still Our Lord showed her the place prepared for her in Hell; not because she deserved Hell, but because, had she not risen from the state of lukewarmness in which she lived, she would in the end have lost the grace of God and been damned. Dignities and Duties of the Priest, 90

In the Great Deluge in the days of Noah, nearly all mankind perished, eight persons alone being saved in the Ark. In our days a deluge, not of water but of sins, continually inundates the earth, and out of this deluge very few escape. Scarcely anyone is saved. Sermons

The saints are few, but we must live with the few if we would be saved with the few. O God, too few indeed they are; yet among those few I wish to be! The Holy Eucharist, 494

We were so fortunate to be born in the bosom of the Roman Church, in Christian and Catholic kingdoms, a grace that has not been granted to the greater part of men, who are born among idolaters, Mohammedans, or heretics. [...] How thankful we ought to be, then, to Jesus Christ for the gift of faith! What would have become of us if we had been born in Asia, in Africa, in America, or in the midst of heretics and schismatics? He who does not believe is lost. He who does not believe shall be condemned. And thus, probably, we also would have been lost. The Incarnation, Birth and Infancy, 153, 156

The common opinion is that the greater part of adults is lost. Preparation for Death, 174

All persons desire to be saved, but the greater part, because they will not adopt the means of being saved, fall into sin and are lost. [...] In fact, the Elect are much fewer than the damned, for the reprobate are much more numerous than the Elect. Preparation for Death, 407-8; The Great Means of Salvation and Perfection, 129

Great Saints

St. Justin the Martyr (100-165): The majority of men shall not see God, excepting those who live justly, purified by righteousness and by every other virtue. Justin: First Apology, XXI

St. Francis Xavier (1506-1552): Ah, how many souls lose Heaven and are cast into Hell! Francis: Letters and Shorter Works

St. Vincent de Paul (1580-1660): Ah! A great many persons live constantly in the state of damnation! Vincent: cf. Voice of the Saints, Francis W. Johnston, London: Burnes and Oats, 1965.

St. Louis Marie de Montfort (1673-1716): Be one of the small number who find the way to life, and enter by the narrow gate into Heaven. Take care not to follow the majority and the common herd, so many of whom are lost. Do not be deceived; there are only two roads: one that leads to life and is narrow; the other that leads to death and is wide. There is no middle way. The Love of Eternal Wisdom, trans. A. Sommers, SMM, Bayshore, NY: Montfort Publications, 1960, p.133

The number of the elect is so small - so small - that, were we to know how small it is, we would faint away with grief: one here and there, scattered up and down the world!

St. John Marie Vianney (1786-1859): The number of the saved is as few as the number of grapes left after the vineyard-pickers have passed. John Mary: GOH p.37

Nothing afflicts the heart of Jesus so much as to see all His sufferings of no avail to so many. Thoughts of the Cure d'Ars, Rockford, IL: TAN, 1984

We shall find out at the day of judgment that the greater number of Christians who are lost were damned because they did not know their own religion. Sermons of the Cure of Ars, page 99.

Lucia Santos of Fatima (1907-1958?): Taking into account the behaviour of mankind, only a small part of the human race will be saved. Lucy: The Secret of Fatima: Fact and Legend, Joaquin Maria Alonso, CMF, Cambridge: Ravensgate Press, 1982, p.106

Taking into account the present development of humanity, only a limited number of the human race will be saved [...] many will be lost. Lucy: Fatima, The Great Sign, Francis Johnston, Rockford, IL: TAN, 1980, p.36

Jacinta Marto of Fatima (1910-1920): "Lucia found Jacinta sitting alone, still and very pensive, gazing at nothing. 'What are you thinking of, Jacinta?' 'Of the war that is going to come. So many people are going to die. And almost all of them are going to Hell." Our Lady of Fatima, William Walsh p. 94; p. 92 in some versions

Great Forgotten Saints

St. Arsenius (Egyptian deacon 345-450) : Brethren, the just man shall scarcely be saved. What, then, will become of the sinner? Arsenius: Life of,

St. Regimius (437-533): Among adults there are few saved because of sins of the flesh. [...] With the exception of those who die in childhood, most men will be damned. Regimus: Book 1 (with Cyprian.)

St. John Climacus (Syrian monk 525-600): Live with the few if you want to reign with the few. John: "Ladder to Paradise"

Blessed James of Voragine (Dominican, 1230-1298): One day, St. Macarius found a skull and asked it whose head it had been. "A pagan's!" it replied. "And where is your soul?" he asked. "In Hell!" came the reply. Macarius then asked the skull if its place was very deep in Hell. "As far down as the earth is lower than Heaven!" "And are there any other souls lodged even lower?" "Yes! The souls of the Jews!" "And even lower than the Jews?" "Yes! The souls of bad Christians who were redeemed with the blood of Christ and held there privilege so cheaply!" The Golden Legend

St. John of the Cross (1542-1591): Behold how many there are who are called, and how few who are chosen! And behold, if you have no care for yourself, your perdition is more certain than your amendment, especially since the way that leads to eternal life is so narrow. John of the Cross: Complete Works

St. Robert Southwell (1561-1595): Oh how much are the worldlings deceived that rejoice in the time of weeping, and make their place of imprisonment a palace of pleasure; that consider the examples of the saints as follies, and their end as dishonourable; that think to go to Heaven by the wide way that leadeth only to perdition! Robert: Letters From the Saints, op. cit. 19

St. John Eudes (1601-1680): Get out of the filth of the horrible torrent of this world, the torrent of thorns that is whirling you into the abyss of eternal perdition. [...] This torrent is the world, which resembles an impetuous torrent, full of garbage and evil odours, making a lot of noise but flowing swiftly passed, dragging the majority of men into the pit of perdition. John Eudes: The Admirable Heart of Mary

Blessed Sebastian Valfre (1629-1710): I fear that Last Day, that day of tribulation and anguish, of calamity and misery, of mist and darkness, that Day on which, if the just have reason to fear, how much more should I: an impious, wretched, and ungrateful sinner! Sebastian: Letters From the Saints, NY: Hawthorne Books, 1964

St. Leonard of Port Maurice (1676-1751): Extracts from his great sermon on The Little Number of Those Who Are Saved: The subject I will be treating today is a very grave one; it has caused even the pillars of the Church to tremble, filled the greatest Saints with terror and populated the deserts with anchorites. The point of this instruction is to decide whether the number of Christians who are saved is greater or less than the number of Christians who are damned; it will, I hope, produce in you a salutary fear of the judgments of God...

First...let us listen to two learned cardinals, Cajetan and Bellarmine. They teach that the greater number of Christian adults are damned, and if I had the time to point out the reasons upon which they base themselves, you would be convinced of it yourselves. But I will limit myself here to quoting Suarez. After consulting all the theologians and making a diligent study of the matter, he wrote, "The most common sentiment which is held is that, among Christians, there are more damned souls than predestined souls."

Add the authority of the Greek and Latin Fathers to that of the theologians, and you will find that almost all of them say the same thing. This is the sentiment of Saint Theodore, Saint Basil, Saint Ephrem, and Saint John Chrysostom. What is more, according to Baronius it was a common opinion among the Greek Fathers that this truth was expressly revealed to Saint Simeon Stylites and that after this revelation, it was to secure his salvation that he decided to live standing on top of a pillar for forty years, exposed to the weather, a model of penance and holiness for everyone. Now let us consult the Latin Fathers. You will hear Saint Gregory saying clearly, "Many attain to faith, but few to the heavenly kingdom." Saint Anselm declares, "There are few who are saved." Saint Augustine states even more clearly, "Therefore, few are saved in comparison to those who are damned." The most terrifying, however, is Saint Jerome. At the end of his life, in the presence of his disciples, he spoke these dreadful words: "Out of one hundred thousand people whose lives have always been bad, you will find barely one who is worthy of indulgence."...

In the time of Noah, the entire human race was submerged by the Deluge, and only eight people were saved in the Ark. Saint Peter says, "This ark was the figure of the Church," while Saint Augustine adds, "And these eight people who were saved signify that very few Christians are saved, because there are very few who sincerely renounce the world, and those who renounce it only in words do not belong to the mystery represented by that ark." The Bible also tells us that only two Hebrews out of two million entered the Promised Land after going out of Egypt, and that only four escaped the fire of Sodom and the other burning cities that perished with it. All of this means that the number of the damned who will be cast into fire like straw is far greater than that of the saved, whom the heavenly Father will one day gather into His barns like precious wheat...

yet I am horror-struck when I hear Saint Jerome declaring that although the world is full of priests, barely one in a hundred is living in a manner in conformity with state; when I hear a servant of God attesting that he has learned by revelation that the number of priests who fall into hell each day is so great that it seemed impossible to him that there be any left on earth; when I hear Saint Chrysostom exclaiming with tears in his eyes, "I do not believe that many priests are saved; I believe the contrary, that the number of those who are damned is greater."...

Listen to Cantimpre; he will relate an event to you, and you may draw the conclusions. There was a synod being held in Paris, and a great number of prelates and pastors who had the charge of souls were in attendance; the king and princes also came to add luster to that assembly by their presence. A famous preacher was invited to preach. While he was preparing his sermon, a horrible demon appeared to him and said, "Lay your books aside. If you want to give a sermon that will be useful to these princes and prelates, content yourself with telling them on our part, 'We the princes of darkness thank you, princes, prelates, and pastors of souls, that due to your negligence, the greater number of the faithful are damned; also, we are saving a reward for you for this favor, when you shall be with us in Hell.'"...

The following narrative from Saint Vincent Ferrer will show you what you may think about it. He relates that an archdeacon in Lyons gave up his charge and retreated into a desert place to do penance, and that he died the same day and hour as Saint Bernard. After his death, he appeared to his bishop and said to him, "Know, Monsignor, that at the very hour I passed away, thirty-three thousand people also died. Out of this number, Bernard and myself went up to heaven without delay, three went to purgatory, and all the others fell into Hell."

Our chronicles relate an even more dreadful happening. One of our brothers, well-known for his doctrine and holiness, was preaching in Germany. He represented the ugliness of the sin of impurity so forceful that a woman fell dead of sorrow in front of everyone. Then, coming back to life, she said, "When I was presented before the Tribunal of God, sixty thousand people arrived at the same time from all parts of the world; out of that number, three were saved by going to Purgatory, and all the rest were damned."

O abyss of the judgments of God! Out of thirty thousand, only five were saved! And out of sixty thousand, only three went to heaven! You sinners who are listening to me, in what category will you be numbered?... What do you say?... What do you think?...

I see almost all of you lowering your heads, filled with astonishment and horror. But let us lay our stupor aside, and instead of flattering ourselves, let us try to draw some profit from our fear.

St. Benedict Joseph of Labre (1748-1783): Yes, indeed, many will be damned; few will be saved... Meditate on the horrors of Hell which will last for eternity because of one easily-committed mortal sin. Try hard to be among the few who are chosen. Think of the eternal flames of Hell, and how few there are that are saved...I was watching souls going down into the abyss as thick and fast as snowflakes falling in the winter mist. Life of the Servant of God, Benedict Joseph Labre

St. Anthony Mary Claret (1807-1870): A multitude of souls fall into the depths of Hell, and it is of the faith that all who die in mortal sin are condemned forever and ever. According to statistics, approximately 80,000 persons die every day. How many of these will die in mortal sin, and how many will be condemned! For, as their lives have been, so also will be their end. Madrid: Library of Christian Authors, 1947.

APPENDIX 7 - STORIES OF MIRACLES

The purpose of this appendix is to show just how important it is to have the Faith and be baptized. Invincible ignorance is the worst kind of handicap. It does not save, but only damns the soul. Baptism of Desire is a real miracle that comes from God, and it is never to be understood as an alternative to Heaven. The Sacrament of Baptism with the Catholic Faith is the only way to Heaven under ordinary conditions. There is no alternative.

One of the great miracles of St. Patrick is recorded in Objection # 3

Perhaps the most extraordinary case of bilocation is that recorded in the life of **VEN. MARY OF AGREDA** (d. 1665), a humble nun who spent forty-six years in the Convent of the Conception in Agreda, Spain. Not only did the Venerable travel mystically across Spain and Portugal, but she also crossed an ocean to visit another continent that was known as America. Her final destination was New Mexico and the Indians of an isolated tribe. The event took place in the following manner. One day in the year 1620, while rapt in ecstasy, Maria was transported to New Mexico, where she was commanded by Jesus to teach the Indians. She spoke in her native Spanish, but was nevertheless understood; she, in turn, understood the language of the Indians. Because they did not know her name, the Indians called her the "Lady in Blue" because of the blue mantle she wore over her habit. When she awoke from her ecstasy she found herself in the convent in Agreda. Two reports of a nun teaching the Indians reached Don Francisco Manzo y Zuniga, Archbishop of Mexico. One report was from Mary of Agreda's own confessor, Fray Sebastian Marcilla, who contacted the Archbishop to learn if Mary of Agreda's report to him that she had bilocated to the Indian territory was correct. The other report came from missionaries who related how the Indians sought them out under the direction of a Lady in Blue. To determine the truth of these reports the Archbishop assigned Fray Alonzo de Benavides of the Franciscan Order to investigate. Fray Benavides was then the director of the missionaries who labored from Texas to the Pacific. One day in the year 1629 Fray Benavides was sitting outside the Isleta Mission when a group of fifty Indians from an unknown tribe approached him and asked that he send missionaries to their territory. In his letters to both Pope Urban VIII and King Philip IV of Spain, Fray Benavides revealed that the Indians had travelled a great distance from a place called Titlas, or Texas, and that they knew where to find the friars from the directions given them by a Lady in Blue who had taught them the religion of Jesus Christ. Two missionaries were sent back with the Indians. These holy men found the Indians well instructed in the Faith and baptized the entire tribe. After searching for eleven years, Fray Benavides finally found the mysterious nun, not in America, but in Spain. On his return to Spain in 1630, he visited the Superior General of his order, Fr. Bernardine of Siena. It was he who told Fray Benavides that the Lady in Blue was Sr. Maria of the convent in Agreda. Realizing that the nun, out of humility, would not reveal her secret to him, the holy nun was placed under obedience to tell all she knew about the visits to America. In the presence of her confessor, Fray Benavides questioned her in regard to the various peculiarities of the province in New Mexico. She described the customs of the different tribes of Indians, the nature of the climate and other details. Fray Benavides later wrote that "she convinced me absolutely by describing to me all the things in New Mexico as I have seen them myself, as well as by other details which I shall keep within my soul." Fray Benavides was later installed as the Auxiliary Bishop of Goa, India. He was ordered by His Holiness Pope Urban VIII in 1634 to write an account of his personal investigations. Of Sr. Mary of Agreda, Fray Benavides once wrote, "I call God to witness that my esteem for her holiness has been increased more by the noble qualities which I discern in her than by all the miracles which she has wrought in America."

The Provincial of Burgos, Fr. Anthony da Villacre, submitted Mary of Agreda to a rigorous ecclesiastical examination. In the end he declared her mystical favors to be authentic. Abbe J. A. Boullan, a Doctor in Theology, wrote of Sr. Mary, "In the highest rank among the mystics of past ages, who have been endowed with signal graces and singular privileges . . . must be placed, without hesitation, the Venerable Mary of Jesus, called of Agreda . . ." Ven. Mary of Agreda bilocated to America during an eleven-year period from 1620 to 1631. She experienced more than five hundred "flights," sometimes making as many as four visits in one day. Mary of Agreda is also the author, with the help of the Blessed Virgin, of The Mystical City of God, which is regarded as the autobiography of the Mother of Jesus.

ST. FRANCIS XAVIER (d. 1552) is regarded as one of the Church's most illustrious missionaries. He was born of noble parents and was by nature refined, aristocratic and ambitious. He was for a time professor of philosophy at the University of Paris, where he met St. Ignatius Loyola and became one of that Saint's original seven followers. His missionary career began in 1540, when he journeyed to the East Indies. Within ten years he had made successful visits to Ceylon, India, Malaya and Japan. He performed many miracles and exercised many mystical gifts, including that of bilocation. He is reported to have been at several places at the same time preaching to the natives. So carefully witnessed were these bilocations and so numerous were they that one biographer admits that the "bilocations which are related in the story of St. Francis Xavier would seem to be of quite ordinary occurrence."

Both stories taken from Mysteries Marvels Miracles by TAN written by Joan Carroll Cruz

Fr. Cohen and the Cure' of Ars

The last moments for Mrs. Cohen arrived on 13 December 1855. Father Hermann was preaching Advent in Lyons at the time and he announced this sad news to his friend in these terms:"God has struck a terrible blow to my heart. My poor mother is dead ... and I remain in incertitude! However we have so much prayed that we must hope that something has passed between her soul and God during these last moments that we cannot know about. ..." We can easily imagine the pain of Father Hermann in learning of the death of his mother. He had so much prayed and so much had prayers said for her conversion, and she came to appear before the tribunal of God without having received holy Baptism! ..." I also have a mother," would he write one day, "I have left her to follow Jesus Christ, she no longer calls me her 'good son'. Already her hair is silvered, already her brow is furrowed, and I am afraid to see her die. Oh! no I would not like to see her die before loving Jesus Christ, and already for many years I await for my mother that which Monica awaited for Augustine..."God seemed to have despised all his prayers and rejected his loving and legitimate desires. His faith and his love were put through a harsh trial. Nevertheless, if his sorrow was deep, his hope in the infinite goodness of God would not allow itself to be struck down. ...Saint Jean Marie Vianney Cure' of Ars short time later, he confided to the Cure' of Ars his disquiet about the death of his poor mother who died without the grace of Baptism. "Hope!" replied the man of God, "hope; you will receive one day, on the feast of the Immaculate Conception a letter that will bring you great consolation."Six years waiting.

These words were almost forgotten, when, on the 8th December 1861, six years after the death of his mother, a Father of the Company of Jesus handed to Father Hermann the following letter.(The person who wrote this letter died in the odour of sanctity; she was well known in the religious and ascetical world by her written works on the Eucharist.)The letter read: On the 18th October, after Holy Communion, I found myself in one of those moments of intimate union with Our Lord, where he made me so feel his presence in the sacrament of His love that Faith seemed no longer necessary to believe him there.

After a short time, He had me hear His voice and He wanted to give me some explanations relative to a conversation that I had had the night before. I remember that, in that conversation, one of my friends had manifested her surprise that Our Lord, who has promised to accord everything to prayer, had however remained deaf to those of Reverend Father Hermann who had so many times addressed Him to obtain the conversion of his mother; her surprise went almost as far as discontentment, and I had had difficulty in having her understand that we must adore the justice of God and not to seek to penetrate its secrets. I dared to ask of my Jesus how it was that He, who was goodness itself, had been able to resist the prayers of Father Hermann, and not grant the conversion of his mother.

This was His (Our Lord's) response: Why does Anna always want to sound the secrets of my justice and why does she seek to penetrate mysteries that she cannot comprehend?

Tell her that I do not owe my grace to anyone, that I give it to whom I please and that in acting in this way I do not cease to be just, and justice itself. But that she may know that, rather than not keep the promises that I have made to prayer, I will upset heaven and earth, and that every prayer that has my glory and the salvation of souls for object is always heard when it is clothed in the necessary qualities. He added: "And to prove to you this truth, I willingly make known that which passed at the moment of the death of the mother of Father Hermann". My Jesus then enlightened me with a ray of His divine light and had me understand or rather to see in Him that which I want to try to relate. At the moment where the mother of Father Hermann was on the point of rendering her last breath; at the moment that she seemed deprived of awareness, almost without life; Mary, our good Mother, presented Herself before Her Divine Son, and prostrate at His feet, She said to Him:

"Pardon and mercy, o my Son! for this soul who is going to perish. Yet another instant and she will be lost, lost for eternity. I beseech you, do for the mother of my servant Hermann, that which you would like to be done for your own, if She was in her place and if you were in his. The soul of his mother is his most precious good; he has consecrated her to me a thousand times; he has consecrated her to the tenderness and solicitude of my heart. Could I suffer her to perish? No, no, this soul is mine; I will it, I claim it as an inheritance, as the price of your blood and of my sufferings at the foot of your Cross." Hardly had the sacred suppliant ceased speaking, when a strong, powerful grace, came forth from the source of all graces, from the adorable Heart of our Jesus, and came to enlighten the soul of the poor dying Jewess; instantly triumphing over her stubbornness and resistances. This soul immediately turned herself with loving confidence towards Him whose mercy had pursued her as far as the arms of death and said to Him: "O Jesus, God of the Christians, God whom my son adores, I believe, I hope in Thee, have pity on me." In this cry, heard by God alone and which came from the intimate depths of the heart of the dying woman, were enclosed the sincere sorrow for her obstination and for her sins, the desire of baptism, the express will to receive it and to live according to the rules and precepts of our holy religion, if she had been able to return to life. This leap of faith and hope in Jesus was the last sentiment of that soul; it was made at the moment when she brought towards the throne of the divine mercy. Breaking away the weak bonds which held her to her mortal casing, she fell at the feet of Him who had been her Saviour (a moment) before being her Judge." After having showed me all these things, Our Lord added:" Make this known to

Father Hermann; it is a consolation that I wish to accord to his long sorrows, so that he will bless, and have blessed everywhere, the goodness of the heart of my Mother and Her power over mine."

Totally unknown to Reverend Father Hermann, the poor invalid who has just now penned these lines is happy to think that she has perhaps spread a little consolation and balm on the still bleeding wound of the heart of this son and priest. She dares to ask the alms of his fervent prayers, and she likes to believe that he will not refuse to one, who, even though unknown to him, is united to him by the sacred bonds of the same faith and of the same hopes. ..."What appears to add great authority to this letter, is that it had been announced six years in advance by the venerable Cure of Ars.

End of translation –

(pp. 126 – 129, *Vie du R.P. Hermann, en religion Augustine-Marie du T.S. Sacrament, Carme Dechausse*, par M. l'Abbe Charles Sylvain, Paris, 1883. From the French life of Rev. Father Hermann, in religion Augustin-Marie of the Most Holy Sacrament, Discalced Carmelite, by Fr. Canon Charles Sylvain, Paris 1883.)

Published with the approbation of and recommendation of His Grandeur Mgr. Gay, Bishop of D'Anthedon, Auxiliary of His Eminence Cardinal Pie, Bishop of Poitier, 4 Dec. 1880 and of His Grace Mgr. de la Bouillerie, the Archbishop of Perga, Coadjutor of Bordeaux, 23 July 1881 of His Lordship Mgr. Adolphe-Louis Perraud, Bishop of Autun and Member of the French Academy, 8 March, 1882 and of the Most Reverend Father Luc of St. John of the Cross, Father General of the Discalced Carmelites, 4 May, 1880) – See more at: http://papastronsay.blogspot.com/2011/10/text-of-letter-prophesied-to-father.html#sthash.wH0Y7xjs.OeWRnA1u.dpuf

See more at: http://papastronsay.blogspot.com/2011/10/text-of-letter-prophesied-to-father.html#sthash.wH0Y7xjs.dpuf

APPENDIX 8 – CASES INVOLVING UN-BAPTIZED INFANTS

The Irish Monk Pelagius was the first to teach that it was possible for un-baptized infants to enter heaven.

St. Augustine countered Pelagius: 'Let no one promise infants who have not been baptized a sort of middle place of happiness between damnation and Heaven, for this is what the Pelagian heresy promised them' (The Soul and Its Origin, *Patrologiae Latinae, Migne*, 44:475).

The Council of Lyons II declared: "The souls of those who die in actual mortal sin, or with Original Sin only, however, immediately descend into Hell, yet to be punished with different punishments." (D 464)

The Council of Florence declared: "Moreover, the souls of those who depart in actual mortal sin or in original sin only, descend immediately into hell but to undergo punishments of different kinds." (D 693)

Pope St. Zosimus solemnly stated: "If anyone says that, because the Lord said 'In My Father's house are many mansions,' it might be understood that in the Kingdom of Heaven there will be some middle place, or some place anywhere, where the blessed infants live who departed from this life without Baptism, without which they cannot enter into the Kingdom of Heaven which is life eternal: Let him be anathema. For when the Lord says 'Unless one be born again of water and the Holy Ghost, he shall not enter into the Kingdom of God,' what Catholic will doubt that one who has not deserved to be a co-heir with Christ will be a partner of the Devil?" (Pope Zosimus at the Council of Carthage XVI, Canon 3, Denzinger, 30th edition, p.45, note 2).

"Anyone who would say that even infants who pass from this life without participation in the Sacrament of Baptism shall be made alive in Christ goes counter to the preaching of the Apostle and condemns the whole Church, because it is believed without doubt that there is no other way at all in which they can be made alive in Christ" (St. Augustine, Epistle to Jerome, Journel: 166).

Baptism of Desire

> **Objection:** Since Baptism of Desire applies to adults, then by that same token the desire of parents to baptize their infants also would apply.

This is the same objection Protestant Reformer and notorious anti-Catholic John Calvin defended.

St. Augustine answered this objection in his Epistle to Boniface: "For it is not written 'Unless a man be born again by the will of his parents' or by the faith of those presenting him or ministering to him,' but of water and the Holy Spirit" (*Rouet de Journel: Enchiridion Patristicum*: 98).

St. Alphonsus Maria Liguori responded with: "Calvin says that infants born of parents who have the faith are saved, even though they should die without Baptism. But this is false: for David was born of parents who had the faith, and he confessed that he was born in sin. This was also taught by the Council of Trent in the Fifth Session, number Four: there the fathers declared that infants dying without Baptism, although born of baptized parents, are not saved, and are lost, not on account of the sin of their parents, but for the sin of Adam in whom all have sinned" (Explanation of Trent, Duffy Co., 1845, p.56).

A Flemish Jesuit named Cornieilis Van Den Steen declared in his Commentaria: "Calvin, in order to detract from the necessity of Baptism, maintains that the children of believers are justified in the womb simply because they are children of believers. But this is absurd and perverse, and condemned by the Church as heretical. If it be lawful to wrest this passage with Calvin, then we may do the same with every other passage, and thus pervert; the entirety of Scripture. No commandment will survive, not even the institution of Baptism itself!" (In John III).

The Council of Florence states, "With regard to children, since the danger of death is often present and **the only remedy available to them is the sacrament of baptism by which they are snatched away from the dominion of the devil** and adopted as children of God, it admonishes that sacred baptism is not to be deferred for forty or eighty days or any other period of time in accordance with the usage of some people, but it should be conferred as soon as it conveniently can; and if there is imminent danger of death, the child should be baptized straightaway without any delay, even by a lay man or a woman in the form of the church, if there is no priest" (Decrees of the Ecumenical Councils Vol.1, p. 576)

The Roman Catechism says baptism for infants should not be delayed "**Since infant children have no other means of SALVATION except Baptism...**" (p. 178)

Again, the Roman Catechism also says adults "are not baptized at once....The delay is not attended the same danger as in the case of infants, which we have already mentioned..." (p. 179)

Notice: The implication is the infants already come from adults who have the Faith, and it is those children that need to be baptized without delay.

However, it's possible that infants can be saved without any remedy whatsoever, if God so desires it. God can save whomever He chooses, however He chooses. Yes, without God's special intervention, there's no hope for the unbaptized infants. We'll simply have to wait to get to heaven to see who actually made it by God's special intervention.

Pope Martin V, Council of Constance, Session 15, July 6, 1415. Condemning the articles of John Wyclif Proposition 6:

"Those who claim that the children of the faithful dying without sacramental baptism will not be saved, are stupid and presumptuous in saying this." Condemned

Baptism of Blood

The Holy Innocents, celebrated on December 28, died morally for Christ, and thus were "baptized in their own blood"; yet they did not need membership in the Catholic Church, which was of a future Testament.

If any infant is martyred for the sake of Jesus Christ or the Faith, he will go to Heaven. SEE OBJECTION 29

Limbo

In his decree against the Synod of Pistoia in 1794, Pius VI alludes to "that place of the lower regions which the faithful generally designate as the limbo of the children" in which the souls of those dying "with the sole guilt of original sin" go. Nevertheless, the view which the Holy Father adopts in no way holds either for a parental or infantile 'baptism of desire' nor for the rewards of the Beatific Vision for unbaptized souls (Denzinger 1526).

This limbo of the children amounts to merely the 'highest place' in the abode of Hell, as explained by St. Vincent Ferrer in his sermon preached on the Octave of the Epiphany (Sermons, London: Blackfriars, 1954, p. 82-83).

In other words, Limbo is Hell but with a different degree of suffering. To say Limbo doesn't exist is to say part of Hell doesn't exist, and that part of Hell has been infallibly defined to exist at Florence by Pope Eugene IV. Those parts of Hell are where those who die in mortal sin or original sin only "under go punishments of different kinds."

> **Objection:** It would be unjust to send un-baptized infants to hell (Limbo). They never had a chance especially those who died in the womb. It's not their fault and they are innocent. Therefore, God must have mercy on them.

We are not born innocent. We have the stain of Original Sin, which we inherited from our first parents. This sin is the state of being absent of Sanctifying Grace, which all men must have to be saved. The Sacrament of Baptism is the new birth, which frees us from sin and restores us in the friendship of God as His adopted sons with Sanctifying Grace.

God is sovereign. Nothing happens without His permission and without His power over it. Yet, He allows infants to die un-baptized. God could have prevented the deaths altogether.

God sees the future and knows everything that will happen. (See I Sam. 23:1-14 RSV, I Kings in DR version) He sees all men and whether they will be saved or be damned. It is quite possible that all un-baptized infants were foreseen to go to the fires of hell. In God's mercy, he allows all those infants to die un-baptized (either naturally or by man) so that their hell will not be so great. Therefore, God does have mercy on them. God could also see the damage such souls might cause for others and is having mercy on those souls too.

Objection: There are far too many infants that die for this to be a reasonable explanation.

Yet, if you read APPENDIX 6, you will see that this is a very reasonable explanation since most everybody ends up in hell anyway.

Why does God have mercy on some and not others in the same way is a mystery.

For my thoughts are not your thoughts: nor your ways my ways, saith the Lord. For as the heavens are exalted above the earth, so are my ways exalted above your ways, and my thoughts above your thoughts. Isaias 55:8-9

APPENDIX 9 - THE HOLY SCRIPTURES ON THE CATHOLIC CHURCH

The purpose of this appendix is to demonstrate using the Holy Scriptures that outside the Catholic Church there is no salvation. (RSV CE Bible is used)

Jesus is the Truth.

(John 14:6) *Jesus said to him, "I am the way, and the truth, and the life; no one comes to the Father, but by me.*

Comment: This implies that apart from the truth is apart from the way and life itself. The "Way" was how the Church was first known. The Way, Truth, and Life are so linked together, that you cannot have one without the others. You cannot have only one part of Christ. You either have Him totally or not at all.

Jesus is King and bears witness to the truth.

(John 18:37) *You say that I am a king. For this I was born, and for this I have come into the world, to bear witness to the truth.*

Comment: Christ bore witness to "the" truth. This means truth is not relative. If it is true for you, it must be true for me.

Jesus said he would build his [one] Church and it will never die.

(Matthew 16:18) *And I tell you, you are Peter, and on this rock I will build my church, and the gates of hell shall not prevail against it.*

(Matthew 28:20) *I am with you all days, even unto the consummation of the world.*

Comment: Notice, Christ built a church, not churches. The 20,000 plus denominations and non-denominations today, do not add up to "a" church. All have different ways, beliefs, teachings, and practices. They all do not make up a single religious church.

The Church is the Body of Christ because She is the Bride of Christ.

(Ephesians 5:22-32) *[22] Wives, be subject to your husbands, as to the Lord. [23] For the husband is the head of the wife as Christ is the head of the church, his body, and is himself its Savior. [24] As the church is subject to Christ, so let wives also be subject in everything to their husbands. [25] Husbands, love your wives, as Christ loved the church and gave himself up for her, [26] that he might sanctify her, having cleansed her by the washing of water with the word, [27] that he might present the church to himself in splendor, without spot or wrinkle or any such thing, that she might be holy and without blemish. [28] Even so husbands should love their wives as their own bodies. He who loves his wife loves himself. [29] For no man ever hates his own flesh, but nourishes and cherishes it, as Christ does the church, [30] because we are members of his body. [31] "For this reason a man shall leave his father and mother and be joined to his wife, and the two shall become one flesh." [32] This mystery is a profound one, and I am saying that it refers to Christ and the church;*

(Colossians 1:18,24) *[18]He is the head of the body, the church; [24] his body, that is, the church,*

(I Corinthians 6:15) *Do you not know that your bodies are members of Christ? Shall I therefore take the members of Christ and make them members of a prostitute? Never!*

(I Corinthians 12:27) *Now you are the body of Christ and individually members of it.*

(Romans 12:4-5) *For as in one body we have many members, and all the members do not have the same function, so we, though many, are one body in Christ, and individually members one of another.*

The Church is the Way.

(Acts 9:2) *so that if he found any belonging to the* **Way**

(Acts 19:9,23) [9] *when some were stubborn and disbelieved, speaking evil of the **Way** before the congregation [23] About that time there arose no little stir concerning the **Way**.*

(Acts 24:14,22) [14] *that according to the **Way**, which they call a sect, worship the God of our fathers, believing everything laid down by the law or written in the prophets, [22] But Felix, having a rather accurate knowledge of the **Way**,*

Comment: If Christ is the Way and the Church is the Way, and the Church is the Body of Christ, then apart from Christ and the Church is apart from Life. Apart from life means apart from salvation, therefore, outside the church there is no salvation.

The Church is Christ's Flock.

(John 10:14-16) *I am the good shepherd; I know my own and my own know me, as the Father knows me and I know the Father; and I lay down my life for the sheep. And I have other sheep, that are not of this fold; I must bring them also, and they will heed my voice. So there shall be one flock, one shepherd.*

(John 18:37) *Every one who is of the truth hears my voice.*

(I Peter 5:1-4) *So I exhort the elders among you, as a fellow elder and a witness of the sufferings of Christ as well as a partaker in the glory that is to be revealed. Tend the flock of God that is your charge, not by constraint but willingly, not for shameful gain but eagerly, not as domineering over those in your charge but being examples to the flock. And when the chief Shepherd is manifested you will obtain the unfading crown of glory.*

Comment: The Church is "of the truth" because it hears the voice of Christ, who is the Head and Shepherd. Again, there is only "one flock" not different flocks. Those who are not of the one flock, Christ must bring into the fold. The implication again, is the flock will attain salvation with the "crown of glory", but outside the fold there will not be that crown of glory meaning no salvation.

The Church is a visible institution.

(Matthew 5:14) *You are the light of the world. A city set on a hill cannot be hid.*

(I Corinthians 12:28) *And God has appointed in the church first apostles, second prophets, third teachers, then workers of miracles, then healers, helpers, administrators, and speakers in various kinds of tongues.*

(Colossians 1:24-25) *his body, that is, the church, of which I became a minister according to the divine office*

Comment: The Church is visible or else these passages are meaningless. It is not some invisible body of true believers only. If there are apostles and they are first, then the rest should follow them because Apostles are leaders, overseers, and the bishops of the Church. They did not appoint themselves but from Christ himself or other Apostles after Him. They don't start their own churches but spread the one Church already founded.

The Church is the household of God.

(Ephesians 2:19-22) *So then you are no longer strangers and sojourners, but you are fellow citizens with the saints and members of the household of God, built upon the foundation of the apostles and prophets, Christ Jesus himself being the cornerstone, in whom the whole structure is joined together and grows into a holy temple in the Lord; in whom you also are built into it for a dwelling place of God in the Spirit.*

(I Timothy 3:15) *you may know how one ought to behave in the household of God, which is the church of the living God*

Comment: Notice, the Church is built upon Christ and the apostles and prophets, not men reinventing religion with a new foundation of enlightened thought such as the Protestant and Evangelical Reformers who started their own churches based on what they thought the church should be. Sola Scriptura (Bible Alone) is the myth, which became the justification to reject the foundation of the

Apostles, and create a new foundation and just call it the foundation of the Apostles. Modernism is the enlightened thought of the new religion of Rome, which replaced historic Christianity and usurped the Catholic name.

The Church is the household of Faith.

(Galatians 6:10) *So then, as we have opportunity, let us do good to all men, and especially to those who are of the household of faith.*

Comment: The Church equals Faith. If you have "the" Faith, you are of "the" Church.

The Church is the one Faith.

(Ephesians 4-6) *There is one body and one Spirit, just as you were called to the one hope that belongs to your call, one Lord, one faith, one baptism, one God and Father of us all, who is above all and through all and in all.*

(I Timothy 6:20-21) *O Timothy, guard what has been entrusted to you. Avoid the godless chatter and contradictions of what is falsely called knowledge, for by professing it some have missed the mark as regards the faith. Grace be with you.*

(Jude 1:20) *But you, beloved, build yourselves up on your most holy faith; pray in the Holy Spirit;*

Comment: Since there is only one Lord, it only follows that there is only one Faith. The Church is the Body of Christ. It equals the Faith, which equals the Way, the Truth, and the Life.

The Church has true authority.

(Matthew 18: 17-18) *tell it to the church; and if he refuses to listen even to the church, let him be to you as a Gentile and a tax collector. Truly, I say to you, whatever you bind on earth shall be bound in heaven, and whatever you loose on earth shall be loosed in heaven.*

(Galatians 1:8) *But even if we, or an angel from heaven, should preach to you a gospel contrary to that which we preached to you, let him be accursed (anathema or cut-off).*

(Titus 2:15) *Declare these things; exhort and reprove with all authority. Let no one disregard you.*

Comment: If you have a disagreement about something of the Faith, which Church do you take it to? If the Faith is the Church, then there must be someone whom has the authority in the Church to say so. This someone is the one who has the authority to bind and loose. He is the one whom has the authority to anathematize. Although several persons could make certain decisions in the Church, it ultimately must come down to one person in the end. But the authority cannot be rejected or else you will automatically be cut-off from the Way. Thus, the rejection of this authority will be the rejection of salvation. "Whoever hears you, hears me; and whoever rejects you, rejects me," says the Lord Jesus. (Luke 10:16)

The Church is immaculate and has no flaws or defections.

(Ephesians 5:25-27) *Christ loved the church and gave himself up for her, that he might sanctify her, having cleansed her by the washing of water with the word, that he might present the church to himself in splendor, without spot or wrinkle or any such thing, that she might be holy and without blemish.*

Comment: This demonstrates how one cannot complain about anything the Church teaches or practices or else the implication would be the Church is not a spotless Bride, but a whore. He who rejects anything the Church teaches or practices because he thinks them to be spots, wrinkles or blemishes of the Church, blasphemes Christ and His Church.

The Church is the pillar and bulwark of Truth and is infallible.

(I Timothy 3:14-15) *I am writing these instructions to you so that, if I am delayed, you may know how one ought to behave in the household of God, which is the church of the living God, the pillar and bulwark of the truth.*

Comment: A pillar and bulwark is something that holds something else up. In this case, it is the Church who holds up the Truth. If something is not true, then it is a lie. The Church cannot lie. Everything the Church teaches must be true or this passage is meaningless.

(John 18:37) *Every one who is of the truth hears my voice.*

(John 4:23-24) *But the hour is coming, and now is, when the true worshipers will worship the Father in spirit and truth, for such the Father seeks to worship him. God is spirit, and those who worship him must worship in spirit and truth."*

Comment: The worship of the Church is of the spirit and truth. It is not apart from the spirit and truth, or else, it would not be the true Church doing the worshiping.

(John 16:7,13) *[7] Nevertheless I tell you the truth: it is to your advantage that I go away, for if I do not go away, the Counselor will not come to you; but if I go, I will send him to you. [13] When the Spirit of truth comes, he will guide you into all the truth; for he will not speak on his own authority, but whatever he hears he will speak, and he will declare to you the things that are to come.*

(John 17:17,19) *[17} Sanctify them in the truth; thy word is truth. [19] And for their sake I consecrate myself, that they also may be consecrated in truth.*

(Matthew 16:18-19) *And I tell you, you are Peter, and on this rock I will build my church, and the gates of hell shall not prevail against it. I will give you the keys of the kingdom of heaven, and whatever you bind on earth shall be bound in heaven, and whatever you loose on earth shall be loosed in heaven.*

Comment: What are the gates of hell but the lies of the devil and men. If the Church taught one lie, then the powers of hell would prevail. However, Christ promised this never to happen. The keys are given to one man, Peter. He is that someone whom Christ has given the power and the authority to bind and loose. He is the one whom has been given the authority to anathematize. The keys also denote succession. All this can be seen in Isaiah 22:22, from which Christ, the Eternal son of David, was drawing from, when He gave Peter the keys, just as Eli'akim was given the key to the house of David.

Therefore, Peter's true successors will have his same power, which ultimately comes from Christ. This has always been the belief and practice of the Church Christ founded. To reject Peter and his successors' authority is to reject the historic Christian faith. It also means the rejection of the Way, the Truth, and the Life who is Christ himself. Apart from this truth of Peter means apart from salvation. Salvation depends on this truth to make sense of the whole of the Scriptures about what the Church is, does, and means. Refusing to listen even to the Church, which must by necessity come down to the authority of one man, is to be as the Gentile and tax collector.

(Matthew 18: 17-18) *tell it to the church; and if he refuses to listen even to the church, let him be to you as a Gentile and a tax collector. Truly, I say to you, whatever you bind on earth shall be bound in heaven, and whatever you loose on earth shall be loosed in heaven.*

The Church guards all truth and keeps out all false teachings.

(Galatians 1:8) *But even if we, or an angel from heaven, should preach to you a gospel contrary to that which we preached to you, let him be accursed (anathema or cut-off).*

(I Corinthians 16:21-23) *I, Paul, write this greeting with my own hand. If any one has no love for the Lord, let him be accursed. Our Lord, come! The grace of the Lord Jesus be with you.*

(II Timothy 4:3-4) *For the time is coming when people will not endure sound teaching, but having itching ears they will accumulate for themselves teachers to suit their own likings, and will turn away from listening to the truth and wander into myths.*

(I Peter 5:8-9) *Be sober, be watchful. Your adversary the devil prowls around like a roaring lion, seeking some one to devour. Resist him, firm in your faith*

(Colossians 1:21-23) *And you, who once were estranged and hostile in mind, doing evil deeds, he has now reconciled in his body of flesh by his death, in order to present you holy and blameless and irreproachable before him, provided that you continue in the faith, stable and steadfast, not shifting from the hope of the gospel which you heard, which has been preached to every creature under heaven, and of which I, Paul, became a minister.*

(John 15:4-10) *Abide in me, and I in you. As the branch cannot bear fruit by itself, unless it abides in the vine, neither can you, unless you abide in me. I am the vine, you are the branches. He who abides in me, and I in him, he it is that bears much fruit, for apart from me you can do nothing. If a man does not abide in me, he is cast forth as a branch and withers; and the branches are gathered, thrown into the fire and burned. If you abide in me, and my words abide in you, ask whatever you will, and it shall be done for you. By this my Father is glorified, that you bear much fruit, and so prove to be my disciples. As the Father has loved me, so have I loved you; abide in my love. If you keep my commandments, you will abide in my love, just as I have kept my Father's commandments and abide in his love.*

(I Timothy 1:3-11) *As I urged you when I was going to Macedonia, remain at Ephesus that you may charge certain persons not to teach any different doctrine, [4] nor to occupy themselves with myths and endless genealogies which promote speculations rather than the divine training that is in faith; [5] whereas the aim of our charge is love that issues from a pure heart and a good conscience and sincere faith. [6] Certain persons by swerving from these have wandered away into vain discussion, [7] desiring to be teachers of the law, without understanding either what they are saying or the things about which they make assertions. [8] Now we know that the law is good, if any one uses it lawfully, [9] understanding this, that the law is not laid down for the just but for the lawless and disobedient, for the ungodly and sinners, for the unholy and profane, for murderers of fathers and murderers of mothers, for manslayers, [10] immoral persons, sodomites, kidnapers, liars, perjurers, and whatever else is contrary to sound doctrine, [11] in accordance with the glorious gospel of the blessed God with which I have been entrusted.*

(II Tim 1:14) *guard the truth that has been entrusted to you by the Holy Spirit who dwells within us.*

CONCLUSION

According to the Holy Scriptures, the Church Christ founded is the household of God and Faith. It is a visible institution with divine offices. It has the full authority of Christ to teach, preach, sanctify, and anathematize. The Church is One, Holy, Catholic, and Apostolic. It is united in faith and perfected in truth. Outside this Church, there is no salvation. The Church of Christ can be found in all generations as Christ promised. Only the Catholic Church can claim to be this Church for She alone has all the marks.

www.ingramcontent.com/pod-product-compliance
Lightning Source LLC
Chambersburg PA
CBHW022006100426
42738CB00041B/685